The Great E

How to buy just about anything and get your money back!

By
Stephen Mycoe BA(Hons) Dhp

All Rights Reserved. Copyright © 2008 Stephen Mycoe BA(Hons) Dhp

Cover Images supply, created and copyrighted by www.UKDesign.net

Book Block Designed by www.**Authordox**.co.uk

No part of this book may be reproduced or transmitted in any form or by any means, graphic, electronic, or mechanical, including photocopying, recording, taping or by any information storage or retrieval system, without the permission in writing from the publisher.

Published by **Authordox**.co.uk

in association with Lulu.com

Although inspired by actual events, the names, persons, and characters in this publication have been altered for the protection and confidentiality of the people involved. Any resemblance to real life people or events is purely coincidental.

ISBN: 978-0-9558533-0-2

Printed in the UK

Book available at www.the-ebay-con.co.uk

www.The-eBay-Con.co.uk

Table of Contents

Introduction 1

GREAT BIG eBay 1

What is eBay? *1*
- EBay Express 4
- How it works 7
- Registration 7
- How to Buy on eBay 8
- Search for a product to buy 9
- Browsing and Searching 10
- Payment 11
- Advanced Search 12
- How to sell on eBay 12
- Relisting items 13
- Setting up a shop 15
- Benefiting from eBay shops 19
- Feedback 22
- Powersellers 26
- Copyright owner abuse and the VeRo programme ... 31

GREAT BIG PayPal – an eBay company 39

What is PayPal? *39*
- Setting up a PayPal account 40
- PayPal Dispute Resolution Process 43
- Verification 43
- Buyer Protection 44

GREAT BIG eBay Rules and how to get around them! ... 47
- Black Market goods 50
- Defective goods 51
- Fee stacking 52
- Misrepresentation 53
- Multiple self bidding (see also shill bidding) 56
- Non-delivery 58
- Non-payment 58
- Shield bidding 59
- Shill bidding 60
- Switching goods 62
- Credit Card fraud 63
- Stolen goods 64
- Other violations 65
- Keyword spamming 65

Links Policy 65
Misleading Titles 66
Payment Surcharges 66
Spam 66
Categorisation of Listing 66
How to avoid it 66
Avoiding General Online Auction Fraud 66
Avoiding Non-Delivery of Merchandise 67

The GREAT BIG eBay Search Engine 69

How to secretly use eBays marketing machine 69
AO- Auction Optimisation 69
Optimising eBay for Google! 72
Driving traffic to your own commercial website 73
User Names 73
Domain name placements 74
Placing penny bids 74
About me page 75

GREAT BIG psychological ways of winning 77

Why people pay more on eBay than a product is worth! 77
Panic buying 77

How to turn buyers into winners. 81
Creating a sense of urgency 81
A Change in Dynamics 82
Market Place Evaluations 83
Profiting from Multiple Sales 85
Virtual self–esteem 88

Psychological of online auction participation 89
Sense of community 89
Addiction to excitement – seller and buyer addiction 90
Competing against rivals 91
Community Status and sense of belonging 91
Friendship 92
Perceptual Value 92
Sellers advantages 93
Selling and Ending items on Thursdays 94
Moulding Kids into crooks 95
Reserve prices 96

The GREAT BIG eBay Hustle - Tricks to make you Rich 99

Private Listing to sell counterfeit products 99
Shill bidding in Private Auctions 101
Create a seller ring to sell fake products 102

Lost in Post scam 102
Getting extra cash from watchers – if they don't bid 103
Feedback Blackmail.. 104
How traders target Power sellers for blackmail 105
Using PayPal to stop a traders income... 106
Feedback 'loading' 107
Poaching bidders... 108
Building an email database 109
Switching products scam... 110
Sniping 111
Selling non-refundable products and services 113
Selling CD's and DVD's... 114
Ten Day Listings 115

The Buyer is King *116*
Stopping a trader from winning a dispute (and getting their money back).. 116
How to win a product at the last minute 116
What to do if you get banned 117
Use someone else's account.. 118
Get a trading assistant.. 118

The GREAT BIG eBay Con - Case Studies and how they do it................... 121
How the author made £450 in one weekend (equivalent to £164,000 per year) with fake software!.. 121
The GREAT BIG eBay DVD rental service! - Cheaper than Blockbuster!.. 123
The GREAT BIG eBay Business Loan! 124
The GREAT BIG interest free eBay personal loan!.......................... 125
Triple your sales and profits from VHS Videos! 127
Free DVD's and your money back!... 128
Making a quarter of a Million a year selling Tony Robbins CD's!... 131

GREAT BIG Hustlers who didn't get away with it - and the mistakes they made.. 133

Nine case studies *133*
16 year old sold £50,000 worth of 'virtual computers'....................... 134
Selling £100,000 of fake goods. 136
Theft charges following eBay scam. 137
Police raid home of alleged eBay thief. 139
What eBay Isn't Telling You 140
EBay account hijacking 142
EBay con man sentenced 143
Huge non delivery eBay fraud 144
Stolen car parts £32,000. 145

GREAT BIG Products you should avoid buying on eBay 147
    PC Scanners and Printers from private sellers 147
    Online Auctioned Cars 147
    Products without a photo 148
    DVD and CD's from private sellers 149
    Electric downloads, Ebooks, PDF's etc 149
    Mobile phones 150
    Things to look out for before bidding 150
    How to keep ahead of the competition 152

GREAT BIG eBay Solutions 157
    Employ more people – they have the funds! 157
    Multiple bidding 158
    Don't get involved in bidding wars 158
    Reducing fraud with Free pictures 159
    Research your product 160
    Alternative Payment Systems 160
    Reduce your reliance upon eBay 160
    Alternative Online Auction Sites 161
    Useful contacts in the event of Fraud against you. 162
    PayPal discussion forums 165
    The Law 166
    Afterword 169
    About the Author 173

Introduction

EBay has a media presence second to none. You can barely turn on a TV show or radio station without hearing its name mentioned. This is a part of the reason I was so shocked when I attempted to increase my online business by joining eBay and selling my products through this medium. I was confronted by some of the most aggressive, dishonest tricksters that I'd ever cared to do business with. None of this activity was ever mentioned in eBay books - not until now!

I had previously enjoyed a good sales record from my own website, where I had been selling Sports Hypnosis CDs for over five years without one complaint. It was a huge shock and disappointment to discover some buyers on eBay wanted to send my products back and receive a refund. I pride myself on the 25% "returned customer" sales that I usually get from my CDs which is an indication of satisfaction, a level of return sales that is virtually unheard of in my industry. So, when a small percentage of eBayers were apparently disgruntled with my product I was keen to get to the bottom of the problem and to rectify it. I am more than happy to replace faulty products, but it seemed that these eBayers were looking for more than just a refund of their money. After several refunds alarm bells began to ring and the 'penny dropped' that perhaps all was not as it seemed!

Without my previous perfect trading history on my own website I may have not been so suspicious. However, it seemed strange that this was only happening on eBay, but not on my websites or other third parties such as Amazon where I also sold CDs and my books.

Following a search engine investigation I discovered the extent that some eBayers tried to defraud new eBay members. It seemed that if you sold CDs or DVDs on eBay they were keen to purchase the product at any price, copy them for either their own use or to resell and claim a refund. A refund being almost automatic from the "Great minds" at eBay and PayPal (an eBay company). This meant eBayers were not only able to buy products and get their money back, but keep a copy of the product as well. Plus if they chose, they could resell and make profits from the product and there was little I could do about this.

Further investigation saw many other scams that were 'allowed' on eBay that the honest trader could do little about. This certainly was not something that eBay's image projects in the everyday world and the media, but it was quite well known in the online market place.

EBay is one of the worlds largest and most profitable websites and in my opinion should be spending more of its turnover on making the site safer for users and battling fraud. EBay likes to be seen doing something, but fails to adequately stop unscrupulous buyers and sellers from, well, plain theft!

> EBay will have you believe that Feedback or a sellers reputation is an indication of their trust worthiness and at the pinnacle are eBays Powersellers who in eBays own words are the pillocks - sorry – 'pillars of our community'.

Feedback is a big part of eBays claim to regulate good trader behaviour. Traders are rated on how they buy and sell with positive or negative feedbacks given depending on the buyers and sellers experience.

My research has discovered that this system is being used to blackmail other traders and you'll read later how feedback is not a true indication of a traders reputation or behaviour *1, it is at best an indication of a traders ability to deliver products quickly, but not the quality of product or service. I have also documented how the feedback system does not discourage buyers from purchasing products from sellers with poor feedback to such a significant degree that a trader will reduce his income. If a trader does reduce his income from a poor reputation on eBay, he has the ability to eliminate this quickly and without financial loss. The only marked influence feedback offers is in the likelihood of sale completion. In other words feedback is far more an indication on whether the seller is likely to actually send the item than it is on the quality of the product.

It is true that most people overstate the quality of their product on eBay but this is not necessarily an attempt at fraud but naive sellers believing they are doing a good job at sales and marketing. There is of course the unconscious agreement from eBay that one can exaggerate product worthiness by their policy and wording in disputes that a product must be 'significantly different than described' for a complaint to be made. In May 2008 the feedback system changed dramatically, in that, sellers are no longer allowed to issue neutral or negative feedback. I suspect this will open up a whole new wave of problems, more on this later.

You'll also see in this eBay book, how eBay is inconsistent in how it treats traders, even feedback criteria is set differently for high volume sellers compared to other eBayers – this in itself can be misleading.

Since John Donahoe was made Chief Exceuative many changes have been made including the feedback system, the closing of eBay express and other areas of the business that I feel will damage eBay.

Leaving the "fraud" itself aside, I have a growing concern for the mental health of a whole new generation being programmed by "dodgy deals and fake" products. This not only allows them to gain an income from being crafty and dishonest, but unconsciously rewards this behaviour. As I have become more and more exposed to the new generation of eBayers who are financially and emotionally rewarded for lying and cheating, I've noticed a new complacency in their attitudes and a misplaced sense of justice. They are becoming desensitised to the emotions many of us have been taught as we grew up. Guilt and a sense of fair play are being pushed aside and replaced with greed and adrenaline rushes instigated by the fight of auction style purchasing.

You'll see in this eBay book, cases studies of eBayers who blatantly do not understand laws of copyright, trademarks or more disturbingly the moral rights of others. I came across a seller who sold me very poor fake copies of an eight CD set of Spanish language learning CD's who, following a request for a refund refused on the grounds that he'd lose money. He offered me an 'up-grade' of another pirated set of CD's instead of a refund. Upon my refusal he became very abusive and claimed a refund would be impossible as I may be copying the CD for distribution myself hence he would lose out. I could not make him understand that he did not own the copyright to the CD's and was not legally allowed to copy, redistribute or sell these products at all. Furthermore it should be of no concern to him what I chose to do with the CD's, if I did decided to illegally copy and sell CDs it was exactly as he was doing - illegally copying and reselling CD's. Nevertheless, he continued to assert that he 'owned' the CD's as I'd bought them from him and me reselling them (which I had no intention of doing) would be in direct competition to his sales!

This attitude has in my experience become the normal attitude of many eBay sellers. Just by illegally duplicating CD's they seem to feel they then obtain the reseller rights. They even have the audacity to place copyright logos on the product, falsely indicating ownership. Talking about incriminating yourself!

> It seems to me if Mensa is the 'High IQ Society' then members of eBay must have earned themselves the 'Low IQ Society' slogan – just by default.

The fact is that eBay is growing so rapidly that at anyone time there are so many 'new users' on the site assuming financial protection, they become easy prey for the hardened eBay vultures that target the less experienced.

It seems to me if Mensa is the 'High IQ Society' then members of eBay must have earned them selves the 'Low IQ Society' slogan – just by default.

One of my reasons for writing this eBay book is to expose some of the tricks used to con the uninitiated. Hopefully through the widespread knowledge of these weaknesses eBay will be forced to address the issues and make eBay a truly safe place to trade. EBay are fully aware of the problems, but appear more concerned about profit than anything else. New users often list items several times without selling them which yields eBay a repeat income. EBay do not make public the amount of items that are listed, but unsold – I would guess that due to the reluctance of sharing this information unsold goods are a huge part of eBays income. In other words perhaps most traders make a loss on eBay!

EBay also only make public their claimed fraud rate of 0.01%. This is the percent of official complaints through their Buyer Protection Programme, not the actual amount of fraud on the site many of which end up not going through the drawn out system of complaints eBay and PayPal offer.

*1. Ginger Zhe. Jin. 'Price, quality and reputation on eBay. – University of Maryland.'

ONE

GREAT BIG eBay

What is eBay?

EBay is an online market place originally founded in 1995 by Pierre Omidyar. It has become a global phenomenon and one of the few international websites that enjoys billions of dollars turnover annually.

Often quoted as being founded as a place for Omidyar's fiancée to trade in Candy dispensers. This was later dismissed as one of eBays many effective PR stunts to create media exposure. *1

Originally the site belonged to Omidyar's Echo Bay Technology Group until it changed its name to eBay in September 1997. Omidyar had tried to register the domain name EchoBay.com but it was already being used by another company. The solution became his abbreviated name, eBay.com.

EBay rapidly expanded and gradually bought out its main competitors which in turn strengthened eBay's market presence. Because eBay was in the online auction business from the start and the fact that it marketed bizarre and newsworthy products to the media it gained publicity rapidly. Over the years eBay has been able to either integrate or purchase (and subsequently close down) many of its competitors ranging from auction sites to online payment companies.

EBay is one of the worlds most successful websites in terms of profit (profits of $310m on turnover of $1.4bn for 2Q 2006), with $9billion worth of trading went on under its roof in that period. *2

In the year 2005 eBay International achieved net revenues of $4.55 billion and net revenues of $6 billion in 2006 and this has only increased year on year. 2007/2008 saw annual revenues of $7.5 USD *4 (£3.8 billion GBP).

EBay has been growing at a rate of 94% annually encouraged by clever marketing and insufficient fraud measures. Its ability to market publicity stories of quirky and sometimes illegal products listed on its site has been the main reason for its success. Certainly few will maintain that the site is better designed or easier to use than its competitors – in fact it is quite a complicated place to trade if you are a newcomer.

Although eBay always removes "inappropriate products" and services from the market place they always seem to be left on long enough for the national papers and TV media to become aware and increase eBay traffic. One such case was the auction of a students 'virginity' which saw global news coverage when the student placed herself up for auction to help supplement her student living. Many days of front page news were enjoyed by eBay, something usually worth tens of thousands of pounds. Although this story was morally and legally dubious (it could be seen as prostitution) the advert was left on long enough for bids to be placed and publicity sought. In fact, if the student in question is to be believed the transaction actually went ahead.

In disputes eBay often refer to their policies and rules on what is and is not allowed to be traded. However, they also defend themselves when criticised for their lack of monitoring with the statement that they are merely a forum for buyer and seller to communicate they are not a place of trade so cannot be held accountable for misconduct.

EBay currently trades in 33 countries with separate websites for most. It has around 20,000 new members per day totaling 78 million active users.

Over 25 Million items are available on eBay at anyone time across a whole spectrum of goods. Anything from tea pots to plant pots. Even products that should in theory not sell well over the internet, such as cars and houses (which common sense would suggest need checking over in person beforehand) thrive in this market place. For instance, eBay Motors sells a car every two minutes generating a GMV turnover of 13.0 billion alone in 2005. *(C2C and B2C, Laudon and Traver 2004 p.784)*

EBay UK (as apposed to eBay.com US site) was not launched until October 1999. EBay.co.uk is the largest e-commerce site (Nielsen Net Ratings, May 2003) in the United Kingdom with in excess of three million items for sale at any given time.

With constant media interest and clever marketing eBay.co.uk enjoys visits from every third internet user in the UK at least once a month. *(Nielsen / Netratings, April 2005)*

In January 2006 eBay UK's audience reached 11.5 million *(Nielsen / Netratings, January 2006)* and they spend more time on eBay UK than any other website. *(Nielsen / Netratings, April 2005)*

EBay UK made $100M revenue per quarter in 2006 and online auction revenues expected to reach $36 billion by the year 2007. *(C2C and B2C, Laudon and Traver 2004, p. 784).*

Canadian, US and UK users are offered free Buyer and Seller 'Protection' Programmes (on qualified listings) both from eBay and PayPal (another eBay company). Seller protection sounds like a good idea but as we will discover later the scheme seems to be marred with problems highlighted by the fact that nearly ninety percent *3 of online auction fraud is conducted by an eBay company. This statistic is justified by eBay spokesman Kevin Pursglove who said. "Overall, fraud on eBay occurs in less than 0.01 percent of its listings. Typically, 16 million items are listed for sale daily on eBay."

Kevin Pursglove's way of justifying this figure with the percentage rate of 0.01 of listings is a shrewd cloud of marketing. If we puff away the mist we can recalculate that as being around 1600 frauds per day just on eBay! A small percentage but still a huge number of dissatisfied customers who are paying you money - eBay.

Sources : Nielson/NetRatings (January 2006) and eBay Internal Data (March 2005). *Outside the U.S.
*1 Cohen, Adam. The Perfect Store. Published by: Back Bay Books (Jun 2003) ISBN: 0316164933
*2 - eBay losing its 'magic', Published Thursday 20th July 2006www.theregister.co.uk – By Andrew Oorlowski
*3 Competition, fraud may harm eBay. Source: www.dfw.com , Star-Telegram.com
 By Wendy Tanaka., July 5, 2003
*4, The Sunday Times, April 20, 2008, by Dominic Rushe.

EBay Express

EBay Express was eBays new site that allowed only new and only 'Buy it now' listings. In other words eBay were trying to get away from the auction style format that they are so well known for. Only retailers whom eBay staff consider fit are given permission to list products on this site.

When I tried to register on eBay Express the staff at eBay didn't even have the courtesy to give me a yes or no, or a reason why I couldn't if that was the case. They merely made excuses to get off the phone with me and said my application was 'pending' or they'd get back to me.

After several months I gave up, realising this was their style of customer service. Perhaps I was not a 'professional' seller in their minds – despite the fact that I had a Retail account with a 'bricks and mortar' whole seller to distribute health products. If they'd asked like other company's do I could have shown proof of Trade invoices.

EBay Express is a site that is trying to solve some of the problems eBay is having with its auction site. For instance, all items are supposed to be brand new. All sellers are supposed to be 'professional' sellers – although this is a very ambiguous term. There are no auction style sales here just 'Buy it Now' style format.

All items have a Seven day return policy and Buyer 'Protection'. EBay have also acknowledged the problems of CD and DVD duplication that we will go into a little further later. Although allowed on eBay Express CD and DVD's are items not liable to the returns policy. There are a few other items also not covered for a returns policy such as; Made-to-order or customised items, Magazines and periodicals. Software and any recordable media that the seal has been broken - obviously due to ease at which digital media can be installed or duplicated.

Although this new policy seems radical by eBay standards these are only rules that 'bricks and mortar' shops always adhere to and most other professional sites like Amazon.com have always offered.

If you are hoping to claim for Buyer Protection you will need to read the EBay Express small print because as expected it varies significantly from eBay and there are several clauses that prevent you from being able to claim as a buyer.

For instance you must pay via eBay express and not eBay itself and you must pay through PayPal but not PayPals 'send money tab' function.

The problem I see with the 'eBay Express Buyer Protection Policy' *1 is similar to the conventional eBay auction sites problems in that although the buyer must send an unwanted item back within seven days, a full refund is only applicable if the seller admits that the buyer returned the product. As many of the sellers are supposed to be 'professionals' by which I assume they mean large retailers the likelihood of items being left on a desk somewhere in the wrong department is high. In this case customer services could quite rightly assume the buyer is pulling a fast one by claiming a full refund and not sending the item back.

I'm just wondering why other retailers don't seem to have these problems? Is it the type of customer attracted to eBay or is it eBays attitude? In my personal experience I have never had any problems with other online shops such as Amazon so why are there so many issues with eBay returns? Are eBay too big?

As of early 2008 eBay Express in the UK were closed down (eBay express USA is still running). Not surprisingly as I see it. EBay seem to missing the fact that their 'bread and butter' clientele are the everyday person on the street which is the foundation that makes up their brand. Trying to create a new site for new businesses is not going to work and if anything it will weaken eBays current brand. EBay have closed eBay Express down however, they don't seem to have learnt from their mistakes. Instead of running eBay Express they are turning the original eBay into a trading place for big business and penalizing the independent trader. This can only mean bad things for eBay. Some of the new problems seem to arise from eBays new chief executive, John Donahoe who started in his role in May 2008. More about this later.

*1 http://pages.express.ebay.co.uk/service/account/purchase_protection_details.html

How it works

To the newbie (newcomer) it is relatively easy to get started on eBay (although it can become very complicated when you delve into its deepest roots) and eBay offer several ways to walk you through the buying and selling processes. New customers are their 'bread and butter' so they want them to sign up and start paying fees as soon as possible! It is the newbie's who make the financial mistakes of poor listing, re-listing, extra fees for unnecessary eBay 'add-ons' etc, etc. So whether newbie's stay as regular traders or not, the mistakes of a high volume of newbie's make eBay a fortune.

It is an unfortunate fact that it is the newbie who often falls pray to the scammer and becomes disillusioned by the site. Seasoned traders quickly become aware of the low moral standards of eBay traders and are able to avoid most of the scams through experience. They will also be fully aware of how to avoid the pit falls that eBay and PayPal themselves instigate.

Registration

To register on eBay simply click on the registration button available on most pages of eBay, fill in your details. Once you have registered eBay will send you an email to confirm that the address you gave is yours and is correct. Then you just follow the instructions given.

Once registered you can begin either searching for a product to buy or list a product you want to sell.

How to Buy on eBay

EBay is predominately known as an auction style website but users are also able to buy and sell in a fixed-price format (subject to qualifying) this sales format accounting for 34% of trading during 2005. This style of purchasing means you can press a button to buy a product at a fixed price immediately rather than waiting up to 10 days for an auction to end.

> And if you think getting blood from a stone taxing – try getting an over payment back from eBay!

Potential customers are able to search eBay without registering but if you want to buy or sell a product you need to register an account.

It's easy to register an account but you need to have a credit or debit card to be confirmed at your registered address if you wish to sell on eBay. To buy on eBay no credit card is required, account confirmation is done through an email account.

If you don't register your credit card and intend making an income from eBay sales you will be restricted to £250 turnover per month. EBay claim registration of bank details is purely a security measure however, if you set up a Direct Debit for monthly payments from your bank account many traders have found that they start paying excessive amounts automatically. And if you think getting blood from a stone taxing – try getting an over payment back from eBay! Contrary to what eBay claim, registration of a bank account benefits eBay in that they can set up automatic payments from your account and in some instances take money without your immediate consent. For instance, if there is a dispute between yourself and a buyer, PayPal have the ability to take money from your bank automatically to refund a buyer even if you object, assuming a Direct Debit is already set up.

You'll also need to register for a PayPal account (this is the main way to exchange money on eBay with over 90% of eBay listings offering PayPal as a payment option) as most trading is done through this company; failure to do so may hinder your sales. This will take anything from a week to a month or so, as PayPal also like to send a confirmation letter to your home address or to make a transaction into your bank. If they make a transaction into your account you'll have to wait for your monthly statement to arrive in order to confirm the transaction. A bit annoying if you were after a specific product and unable to purchase due to the delay of account set-up however, this is done as a security measure. More on this in the PayPal section.

Over 30% of new eBayers buy on eBay before they venture into selling [2] this may seem to be an attempt to get comfortable with the site but many use it for more sinister reasons. EBayers will often 'buy their reputations' on eBay which essentially means that they will buy lots of cheap products so that their feedback ratings look good before they attempt selling, this could have an effect of giving a fraudster a false reputation of being law abiding before he attempts to con his victims. More about this later.

[2] The Dynamics of seller reputation: Theory and Evidence from eBay p38.

Search for a product to buy

You can make a general search or an advanced search. The advanced search is useful if you want for instance, to search for products in your local area. This is important if the product you are after is too bulky to post or it's something you want to give the once over before bidding such as a car. The advanced search also has a facility that I believe is the most exciting aspect of eBay, that is the 'completed listing' click box we will discuss this a little later. Which enables you to check what already sells on eBay and for how much.

There are two main ways to find a product on eBay;

Browsing and Searching

Browsing: To browse all the categories click the Browse button on the navigation bar and a full list of categories will be displayed. Click on the category that you are interested in and keep on clicking categories until you narrow it down to a specific product that you are seeking.

Clicking or unclicking the 'search title and description' click box may increase or decrease the amount of searched products that you receive.

Searching: If the browse option seems too long winded, you might like to search by typing in keywords in to the search box. You may need to try a couple of different keywords depending on the product you are after. Sellers list with various keywords depending on how they wish to market their product.

For more advanced search options do the same thing but first click the blue hyper link text worded 'Advanced Search' next to the search box or in the search link in the navigation bar. This will bring up lots more options for you to narrow down the search, such as price, location etc.

You will then be faced with a selection of products that should match your criteria although this depends upon how well sellers have listed their items.

- To refine your selection of products, select a Category.
- Check the products description, price (not forgetting to check postage)
- Check feedback and other items sold by seller.
- Place a bid or buy it now – depending on how the item is listed.

Payment

After you have won or purchased an item on eBay you may be prompted to pay immediately using eBay's PayPal payment system or you may be emailed an invoice from the seller quoting how much you owe including Postage. EBay will always send you an email confirming what you have purchased.

Some sellers may request payment via cheque or postal order. This is rare and as we will see later this could be a fraud technique.

No experienced seller will send an item unless they have received payment or received and cleared the cheque that you have been sent. So be aware...

Many con men will delay sending a cheque for several weeks in the hope that you will dispatch your sold item before they send the cheque. They will then not send the cheque and claim it must have been lost in the post. Always wait for payment this includes time for cheques to clear.

E-Cheques are electronic cheques that many people try to trick you with. These work in the same way that a normal cheque will work in the sense that it takes seven days to clear. The difference is that it goes immediately (electronically) into your payment account. This fools many people into sending an item before it has cleared.

Cheques are a great way of receiving funds through eBay because they save you money, if you use PayPal you will be charged a fee, with cheques you usually don't. Having said this eBay transactions are largely completed using the PayPal system and because PayPal ban other systems such as they allegedly did with Googles payment service it is unlikely you will ever see another quick way to pay on eBay.

Advanced Search

The advanced search has a facility that is the most useful aspect of eBay, which is the 'completed listing' click box we mentioned earlier. By enabling you to search items that have sold recently, how much they sold for and in which category, you can keep up with market trends and only sell what's hot or discover products that are not yet on eBay.

Personally when I find a cheap source for a product I always check this search facility before I buy the trade product. I want to know if it sells and if so, how many are sold daily and for how much. If hundreds a day sell for a higher price than I can source them, it's a product I might want to stock.

EBay also offer a paid for service that gives traders access to eBay market trends. These start at £30 per month and go up to hundreds of pounds per month. Personally I think the 'advanced completed listings' search facility is adequate – and free!

How to sell on eBay

EBay walks you step-by-step through the selling process (this is the main way they make their money, they don't charge buyers only sellers) but there is an element that you will need to be aware of; Categorisation.

EBay offer you a 'category suggestion tool' when you begin to list your item. This is in theory a way to simplify and speed up your listings on the site. Try to avoid this- you'll find no hardened eBayer using such a tool as it can incorrectly categorise *1 your item at least a quarter of the time. Always list items manually.

If in doubt search for items similar or the same as you have which have already sold in the advanced search- complete items facility. Find the item that sold for the best price or received the most visitors and catorgorise yours the same way.

Again eBay makes money out of sellers not buyers. Essentially eBay could make extra money if you list in the WRONG category – most often you will list again if you do not sell your product – this way eBay make money out of YOU twice. Not to mention that many people add extras the second time to encourage a sale, such as listing promotions that cost you more. **So get it right the first time!**

Relisting items

One often overlooked aspect that remains a credit to the eBay system is the 'Free' relisting that is offered if your product does not sell. This is if you list your shop product into an auction or buy-it-now format. When the time has elapsed and you have not sold the product you are offered the possibility to relist without the addition of another fee. Hang on a minute, before you rush of and click a hundred items for relisting there is a catch. Yep, eBay in their usual manner have made the process as complicated as they can. And in doing so confuses sellers so that they undoubtedly relist incorrectly and fail to gain the intended credit. The catch is that if you want to relist 'for free' you have to pay the listing fee up front and only get it back if your item sells the first time you relist it! Essentially if your item does not sell the first time that you list it you can relist the item. If it does sell the second time (the first relisting), eBay will refund the Insertion Fee for the relisting, if it does not sell the second time eBay keep the fee. *Are you keeping up*!

This means eBay keeps your money for a further 10 days and collects the interest until it decides to reinstate the money - but only if your item does sell. In short for the duration of the relisting eBay hold on to two listing fees – the original fee and the relisting fee.

It has become clear if you take notice of the eBay forums about this issue many people become overwhelmed by the administration involved in claiming money back or merely checking that one has been reimbursed so it seems most traders don't bother. There are so many pit falls to a free re-listing that it really is not worth worrying about. Just re-list the products you want to and hope that perhaps a fee will be automatically refunded. But remember you have already paid through the shop and again when sending the product to the auction – so it's fair you don't pay again!

Thirdly don't forget you must pay a monthly fee from your shop. This is quite high when you consider the hosting of your own independent website might cost around £6.00 per month. Nevertheless eBay will furnish you with a large client base of people ready to buy.

Eligibility criteria for the credit:

- You must relist the item within 3 months of the original auction end.
- It must be the first re-list of your item, future re-listings will not be refunded.
- If the relisted item does not sell the second time, eBay keep the insertion fee.
- Shop Inventory Format can not be re-listed.
- The price for the relisted item must not increase the second time.

Setting up a shop

Shops are a convenient way to list multiple products long term. In theory, shops are more cost effective as you will gain more exposure for your products. This might be the case. The problem arises if you do not keep tabs on these products. You could be losing money as your product will be renewed every 30 days and you will be billed for every automatic renewal.

Shops used to be an effective source of income on eBay, especially if you (as most eBayers do) specialise in a specific type of product. If for example, you had an auction for a 'Clay Pigeon shooting Hypnosis CD', and an athlete who did not shoot clay pigeons but did target shoot, they might decide to search the sellers other items in his shop and in doing so find the title he wished to purchase.

It used to be fairly cost effective to own an eBay shop, however in August 2006 the great collective minds at eBay reduced the visibility of Shop Listings and introduced a new (more expensive) billing procedure. It seems 6 billion annually is not enough turnover!

My eBay shop went from earning a passive income of at least £1600 per month (not including auction items or sales directed to my website via eBay) to nothing! This was purely due to the reduction in shop inventory exposure. EBay no longer wanted shop inventory listed among the other auctioned products because sellers were leaving multiple products in their shops and when sold eBay received a fraction of the commission compared to auction/buy now listed products.

Now you will only have your shop inventory listed among the auctioned and 'buy it now' listings if the buyers search returns only a small number of products. Any search that returns multiple items ceased to list shop items. What this means is that shop owners are now forced to increase their spending by continuously listing their shop inventory in auction style sales rather than leaving them almost inactively in their shops with fees of only pennies per month (not including the monthly shop fee).

EBays justification for this is as expected profit orientated.

During 2005 and 2006 more than 80 percent of eBay's U.S. merchandise listings shifted from auction style listings to shop store listings, which is more cost effective for the seller.*2 With the majority of product listings making up the minority of profit margins eBay were keen to re-address this statistic with a price hike - we are yet to see whether this will work out in eBays favour. Personally, this has led to me closing my shop. (actually eBay closed it for me but more about that later)

One other reason for the structure change (other than eBay profit) seems to be eBays new eBay Express website. As discussed earlier.

The price rise is said to have cost a lot of people their eBay businesses or at least dramatically reduced their profit margins. In fact this one act has seen an army of disgruntled eBayers from a coalition of protesters seeking a viable eBay alternative that will be loyal to their cause. These eBay customers have arranged eBay strikes to hammer home their protests – with little effect so far on eBays attitude.

One such group threatened a week long boycott of eBay. Twenty Four Thousand protesters signed a petition. In their defense during January 2005 *3 a month before a fee hike, eBay actually took some notice of the eBay community by reducing some of its planned fees to US and Canadian traders.

The truth is eBay still hold a monopoly in the online auction business hence they can currently act as they wish with little reprisal. Even if their customers are upset, if they gain an income from eBay there is no alternative website. Either accept eBays behaviour or give up your trading and income. Following the reduction in shop inventory exposure and the price hike, today you will be billed monthly per product with the addition of a percentage taken from your sale price– nothing unusual there. But the new system has a specific scale of prices that relate to the cost of the product that you list. Even worse; if you sell a mobile phone you are drastically being penalised with huge costs (relatively).

In simple terms if you sell a product such as a £32.00 sports hypnosis CD as I did in my shop, you will now incur several fees. 1; a monthly subscription fee of £6.00 per month, 2; a shop fee of £0.07 pence per month per product (depending on the product price), then 3; 10% of the initial sale price of each product for the first £4.99 plus 8% of the initial £5.00 - £9.99 plus 6% of the remaining selling price balance, (depending on the price of your product). In my case this equates to an over all fee of £3.29 per CD if I sell one directly from my shop without going to auction and not including the monthly subscription. This may not sound like much, but I would have 100 CD's in the shop plus most would need to go to auction to get them in front of eBay customers. I would also need to add fees for having a picture as this is essential. We have not mentioned that there is also a fee from PayPal for processing each transaction. The fee system seems to be deliberately complicated. Just a quick look through the forums on search engines show how many traders are unaware of how much they are being billed and complain that their bills are more than they actually spent. The multiple percentages above make it almost impossible to calculate each product you have and opens up the possibility of being over billed substantially.

It had become impossible to sell shop inventory from my store because there was too much competition in the categories which are usually sports related thus, my shop products were not listed. This forced me to list my products in a fixed price or variable auction format rather than my shop. This too will cost me more both financially and time wise. In fact it is now impossible to list all of my products from my own website on eBay as I now have nearly 100 separate Sports Hypnosis CDs available. As sport is a popular category having shop exposure is impossible for me.

From 21st August the following changes were made to Shop Listings

Shop Insertion Fees.

Insertion price	30 day listings	90 day listings	Good 'Til Cancelled
£0.01 - £4.99	£0.03	£0.09	£0.03/ 30 days
£5.00 - £9.99	£0.05	£0.15	£0.05/ 30 days
£10.00 - £49.99	£0.07	£0.21	£0.07/ 30 days
£50.00 - £499.99	£0.09	£0.27	£0.09/30 days
Over £500	£0.11	£0.33	£0.11/30 days

At the same time the following changes were made to Shops Listings Final Value Fees.

New Shops Final Value Fees

Insertion price	30 day listings	90 day listings	Good 'Til Cancelled
Item not sold	No Fee		
£0.01 - £4.99	10% for the amount of the selling price up to £4.99		
£5.00 - £9.99	10% of the initial £4.99 plus 8% of the remaining selling price balance		
£10.00 - £49.99	10% of the initial £4.99 plus 8% of the initial £5.00 - £9.99 plus 6% of the remaining selling price balance		
£50.00 - £499.99	10% of the initial £4.99 plus 8% of the initial £5.00 - £9.99 plus 6% of the initial £10.00 - £49.99 plus 4% of the remaining selling price balance		
Over £500	10% of the initial £4.99 plus 8% of the initial £5.00 - £9.99 plus 6% of the initial £10.00 - £49.99 plus 4% of the initial £50.00 - £499.99 plus 2% of the remaining closing value balance		

eBay.co.uk

*1 'eBay wants your money', Terry Gibbs, http://www.auction-revolution.com/system.shtml

*2 eBay Profits Up -*Profits, sales up, amid concerns about growth. October 18, 2006,* http://www.redherring.com, Contact the writer: WTanaka@RedHerring.com

*3 www.Theregister.co.uk

Benefiting from eBay shops

One huge benefit of having an eBay shop is that it gets your products quickly (and temporarily) into Google searches. For instance, take the example of the Sports Hypnosis CD's from my website (www.SportsHypnosis.co.uk). This site is in the top position in every major search engine in the world for its main keyword. However, not every potential buyer of this product types in 'Sports Hypnosis' as a keyword into a search engines. This means that I am potentially losing out on people who type in other relate terms such as 'sports psychology' or 'sports coaching'. In addition there are times when a seasonal event occurs such as the London Marathon where one might be in need of short term exposure to a market place within Google.

Search engine advertising is often expensive so my next best option is to list my 'Easy Marathon' Sports Hypnosis CD onto my eBay shop which then lists the product high up in Google. When someone searches with keywords that match my eBay listing title this will come up relatively high in Google. This is a great way to market specific products into Google.

You must be aware that it only works in shops because all other eBay listings are for a maximum of ten days which is a problem as search engines up-date their listings generally on a 30 day rota. So you need to either happen to have a listing on when Google crawls the web or exceed 30 days to keep your listing up-dated.

If you don't have a shop the other way to have your eBay listing included in Google searches is paying for an eBay 'featured listing' which costs nearly £10 and places you at the top of the eBay page that you listed on until your listing ends. These currently list at the top of Google for the keywords in the listing title. More about this in Chapter Four.

This technique may not continue because of the widely speculated conflict between Google and eBay. Google having applied for a US Patent (Application No. 20040122811) [1] for what they have termed a new type of payment system. Furthermore some online retailers begun testing a Google payment system during early 2006 named GBuy. EBay have been said to have banned the use of Google's payment system from eBay as it competes with eBays PayPal system. So it's debatable how long Google will continue to list eBay items in its search engine- guess it's all down to how mature they are going to be about it? Google were once rumoured to be working on their own version of eBay which could have been a godsend because of the monopoly that eBay commands. Some healthy competition from another online giant would be beneficial all around. Unfortunately, the rumours were quashed with another Google and eBay deal.

Having said this early 2007 saw the advent of Googles final payment system go live 'Googlecart' with no commission for the whole of 2007 and very low commissions promised in the years following. This is hopefully the first step towards the launch of a Google auction site to rival eBay.

It is reported *2 that eBay and Google have settled on a deal that will see eBays listings and adverts high in Googles rankings which keeps eBays traffic substantial.

The deal reported that during mid 2007 the two internet giants will share revenue on search-related text ads delivered on UK eBay sites. It also reports that the emergence of 'Internet voice technology' in online advertising will also see a collaboration between the two companies.

The eBay advertising for the US had already been sewn up by Yahoo, which seems to put eBay in a win/win situation. With the continued battle between search engines sooner or later one will either take a majority market control internationally or even more likely, when you consider online corporate history; one will be bought out by its competitor. Either way eBay has the technology in place with both 'teams' to ride any possible future drop in a market share. In my opinion this is typical eBay business strategy, with little 'loyalty' to any party – just tough business lines.

*1 http://news.zdnet.co.uk, Stefanie Olsen CNET News.com, Published: 29 Aug 2006 11:50 BST
http://news.zdnet.co.uk/internet/0,1000000097,39281969,00.htm

*2 Ecommerce - June 21, 2005 'Google Moving Forward on Payment System' By Susan Kuchinskas. -http://www.internetnews.com/ec-news/article.php/3514551

Feedback

Feedback is supposed to represent an eBayers buying/selling reputation, in other words the person is rated by the service that they provide. Feedback is the number that can be found next to an eBayers user ID. Although the way feedback is displayed changed slightly in February 2007 little change has been seen in the ease at which traders can manipulate transactions.

Feedback claims to promote trust between buyers and sellers however, as we will discover this is a hugely misleading aspect of eBay. Feedback can falsely give the impression of a trustworthy seller when in fact there are multiple ways to keep your feedback healthy whilst also either conning people out of their products and/or money or simply giving a very poor service. May 2008 saw changes to the feedback system that claims to solve these problems, more about this later.

The 'normal' trader will use feedback as an incentive to be honest and build up a sense of pride in trading well. The eBay con-man will use feedback as a means to 'blackmail' other traders into giving in to their demands.

Feedback also acts as a mark of distinction to the unscrupulous who delight in getting away with conning and thieving from the less experienced whilst simultaneously enjoying large financial incomes and keeping an apparently good reputation.

You'll find later in this book a technique that allows you to feed hundreds of good feedback comments into your account so that poor feedback is relegated to the back pages. You'll also see how human behaviour predicts that feedback reputations actually do the opposite of what they are intended or claimed to do.

Research has discovered that although there is only a slight effect upon a sellers sales following a negative feedback it is the seller themselves who instigates that trading reduction not the buyers comments. *1

As previously stated, in February 2007 the feedback system changed again and it now shows within the sellers 'feedback profile' the name of the items sold, title and the sale price. You can now also see a 'Detailed Seller Ratings' section where a trader is rated with five rows of 'golden stars' (clearly somebody at eBay experienced a lack of 'Golden Stars' during Kindergarten!) that also represent a traders reputation – each star representing a separate area of the transaction i.e. postage costs, speed in delivery etc (see diagram1 below). This, I predict is going to cause many problems for sellers who often discount their products for a quick sale. For example on occasions I might sell a Sports Hypnosis CD at auction for a starting price of 99 pence just to get some extra interested parties looking at my products and my own linked website. Although I do not do this very often the problem arises because I usually sell my CD's for £32.00 each. If the auctioned item sells for much less than that, say £10.00, whenever I list another product for £32.00 and the potential buyer checks my feedback and notices that I sold a similar item for a third of the price only days ago, they are going to either want a discount or feel that my 'Buy It Now' price is too high and forget my auction altogether. This will not be good for business.

Diagram1

Detailed Seller Ratings (since March 2007)

Criteria	Average rating	Number of ratings
Item as described	★★★★★	24
Communication	★★★★★	24
Dispatch time	★★★★★	24
Postage & packaging charges	★★★★★	24

This change in adding product title and prices to the feedback page is not particularly dramatic, but does have a huge impact on sales if you want to occasionally discount a product. If you do sell a product for a low price I can virtually guarantee buyers will want a similar discount every time. And that is often just not feasible. I think a point that is significant about this change is the advent of eBay Express that sells only new products from registered companies. I can see the benefit to eBay if they can separate normal part-time eBay sellers on their original site with retail companies who will feel the need to move to the eBay express site if discounts are forcing them to stop selling on eBay; perhaps this is the idea?

The other issue with this new 'star' rating feature is; one that it is optional hence, does not represent a true value. Particularly as it is human behaviour to go out of ones ways to rate someone when one is annoyed. Two; it only allows buyers to rate sellers and the buyer remains anonymous. This will see vindictive traders giving good feedback in order to receive good returned feedback but secretly issuing bad star ratings because no retaliation is possible.

On the plus side I assume that by the addition of the star system eBay were trying to sort out the problem they have with sellers inflating postage costs to gain extra profit from their items. This perhaps may benefit eBay trading in the long run however, I doubt it.

More recently eBay have added the feature that if you put negative or neutral feedback for a trader it asks you additional questions. Questions along the lines of why you are leaving poor feedback. One question is 'was the product counterfeit'. This offers the buyer the opportunity to tell eBay the seller is dodgy but not making the seller aware that they have done so. This is eBay actually doing something right in that if a seller gets lots of counterfeit claims in this way eBay can be made aware of it. Whether this works is an issue eBay must answer. Having said this, we may see those sad bitter eBay traders making false allegations just to get kicks without any come back.

May 2008 saw Feedback change even more dramatically with the abolishment of sellers being able to leave negative or bad feedback. With only Buyers being able to leave comments the flood gates will open to the malicious trader that eBay seems to attract. I can see law suits in the future from businesses who do not appreciate slanderous comments that damages their companies brand. To be honest, I feel this feedback change will have to be reinstated, it can't possibly work. The system seems to have been devised to stop feedback blackmail however, there is of course, nothing to stop a buyer from emailing a trader with threats of poor feedback if they do not adhere to their demands. And if the buyer threatens off eBay (which they can do as they are often given private contact details after a transaction) there is no proof. Add to this the fact that if a buyer fails to leave feedback within a few days of receiving the item many hardened eBayer will understand silence is a form of threat. Often traders will be glad to offer an incentive to receive good feedback especially now that eBay have allowed multiple feedbacks from the same trader which it did not allow before May 2008.

*1 'Price, quality and reputation on eBay – Ginger Zhe. Jin, University of Maryland.'

Powersellers

Powersellers are the 'top sellers' of eBay with a high level of feedback (98% positive or better with at least 100 feedbacks). You are automatically offered Powerseller status if you reach specific thresholds. To qualify at the lowest level of Powerseller you will need to sell on average £750 worth of merchandise for three months consecutively from a minimum of 4 items or by selling 100 items per month, without a required monetary value. You will also need to "Not have violated any severe policies" in a 60-day period.

When I say severe policies, eBay has some strange ideals and do set out what constitutes a misdemeanor for a Powerseller. In line with eBays apparent policy of treating different traders differently, or as I like to see it being prejudiced against the majority of eBayers they allow more misdemeanors for the higher the rated Powerseller. This I suppose they justify is due to some traders selling more thus undertaking more transitions. However, if they are said to be the epitome of good trading surely they should do "No wrong" - Why allow any rule breaking?

> The interesting thing about Powersellers is that eBay seem to treat them as higher citizens or more to the point seems to treats other eBayers as second class citizens.

There are two main reasons I say this. *One;* Powersellers have a different (more lenient) system of feedback which helps them gain sales and high amounts of ratings. *Two;* Powersellers have a dedicated Account Manager who assists them in all sorts of ways. In fact it is my opinion that these Account Managers side with the Powerseller in disputes, business transactions and any number of other favorable instances. Three; the higher 'ranked' you are as a Powerseller the more 'illegal' activity you are allowed. See policy below.

Powerseller marketplace compliance policy.

Bronze	4 offences in every two months
Silver/Gold	5 offences in every two months
Platinum	6 offences in every two months
Titanium	7 violations in a 60-day period

The above chart shows the inconsistency in rules for not just ordinary traders but different levels of Powerseller. Depending on your status you are allowed to break the rules in varying degrees. Although some could argue that some sellers have higher sales thus the percentage of rule breaking is lower it doesn't get away from the fact that some traders are allowed to violate rules.

My personal opinion is that often eBay Account Managers help out their clients (Powersellers) more than one would hope. For instance one of the most profitable times of year for eBay is pre and post Christmas – understandably. However, it seems that some smaller traders are suspended over this period to the benefit of higher volume selling Powerseller. Now there could be more than one reason for this.

But my experience points to the reason being that smaller sellers who are treading on a Powersellers "market" and therefore affecting the Powersellers income are suspended for minor reasons. This theory was highlighted to me during the Christmas of 2007.

I had begun selling wholesale Performance supplements and training accessories to complement the sales of my sports hypnosis CD's. I wasn't the only one who'd tapped into this lucrative market and prices started to fall due to the increase in competition. Nothing unusual there – a bit of healthy competition. Wholesale prices of supplements are relatively static so it was difficult to differentiate one product from another. As many people on eBay are unconcerned about buying from powersellers or other eBayers this wave of competition was clearly hitting powersellers who probably only have this sole source of income. One reason I could easily out sell Powersellers was that I sold the same supplements as they did with a similar profit margin but I was able to add a Sports Hypnosis CD with the supplement which gave me an edge.

A couple of months prior to Christmas my business on eBay was starting to get very profitable and I was looking forward to the Christmas rush as we entered November. It was then that I was suspended from eBay for a very minor misdemeanor, a misdemeanor I had conducted many times over several years. That was OK, I broke a minor rule and was suspended for a short period. However, a colleague was also selling my stock from his eBay account. You guessed it, an undisclosed member of the eBay community had allegedly made a complaint about his account and suspended him too. His "misdemeanor" was that his user ID was also a website address – which is not strictly allowed although hundreds of eBayers do this. In fact many eBayers would not trade if it were not for the additional traffic that eBay unofficially diverts to their own websites.

Alarm bells rang because advisers at eBay had suspended me for other reasons although I had a website address as my User Name also. I had SportsHypnosis_co_uk clearly my personal website address, if you replace the underscores with a dot, of which I had been using for years as my eBay address. Add to that the fact that I had emailed and sent my user name to Customer Services on many occasion and nothing was said. In fact even after my suspension was lifted (surprisingly after Christmas!) the customer advisers who reinstated my account still said nothing and I continued to use this User name to this day.

The aspect that also confirmed my suspicions about powersellers was that as soon as I was suspended I noticed many others were also suspended and to my surprise a apparent Powerseller 'price fixing' market emerged. The majority of people now selling the products I was suspended for all began raising their prices and left them higher than before. Surely this was a Customer Adviser plan to help his (paying) client maximise profits over this lucrative period? It does make me wonder if these powerseller advisers are on commission? Clearly this is just an observation of mine, and in someway speculative, but based on experience. We will of course, never find out if this is true from eBay and the statistics of many aspects of eBay trading are not available. But anyone can watch out for this sort of activity.

The New eBayer is someone most susceptible to the misinterpretation of Powerseller feedback. Often they will be impressed by the amount of feedback blissfully unaware that it is calculated differently from theirs, plus not realising how many unsatisfied customers some of them have.

One problem with high turnover Powersellers is that although they keep their feedback over 98% this could still mean that 40 odd customers per month are dissatisfied with the product or have not received anything.

Imagine if you had 40 upset customers every month in a bricks and mortar shop!

Percentage wise it looks insignificant, but you can never account for so many upset customers. That is more than one angry customer per day – clearly the Powerseller in the example is unable to cope with this level of sales. With hundreds who leave a neutral rating that makes no difference to feedback. See example below.

This is one reason why it is often better to buy from someone who does not sell as much as they are often better able to cope with their work load and perhaps more likely to get back to you if there is a problem.

Member Profile: **Halfwit_nutrition** ☆ (15313) **Power Seller**					
Feedback Score:	15313	Recent Ratings;	Past 1 Month	Past 6 Months	Past 12 Months
Positive Feedback:	98.9%				

Members who left a positive:	15477	positive	3029	14397	20393
Members who left a negative:	167	neutral	51	255	309
All positive feedback received:	21777	negative	41	150	187

The beginning of 2008 saw Powersellers being given even more rights over other traders. EBay is now offering PowerSellers fee discounts if they have high ratings, and using the ratings to improve search results for their products. These are based on the new Detailed Seller Ratings (DSR).

If a trader maintains a DSR above 4.6 they will qualify for the 5% discount and in some cases more. See the chart below. To establish your DSR simply 'mouse over' the star in your ratings and a score out of five will be shown. Each star has it's own rate.

Powerseller level	Discount
Titanium	**40%**
Platinum	**35%**
Gold	**30%**
Silver	**25%**
Bronze	**20%**
Non PowerSeller	**20%**

Copyright owner abuse and the VeRo programme.

In theory only copyright owners or legitimate authorised retailers can resell multiple products or use their Trademarks.

On eBay copyright owners have the right to stop another person selling a product if they deem it in breach of copyright laws through the VeRo program. There are 17,000 *1 rights owner registered with eBay. In most cases you are able to sell counterfeit products freely as long as no-one complains, even in this eventuality you are usually only punished with the refund of the value of one or two products. But as your profit in counterfeiting is high it makes little impact on your income.

Through the VeRo program the 'general' eBayer does not have any right to make a copyright infringement claim even if it's obviously a fake product being listed. Claims have to come from the copyright owner and they have to be registered with eBay to make complaints. The general public may only complain about a single dodgy product that they purchased and claim for a refund.

It is more than obvious which sellers duplicate and sell copywritten and counterfeit products on eBay. EBay would be stupid to claim that they are unaware of this. When £3500 computer software packages are being sold for £15 (something that I investigated myself whilst researching this book *2), you know there is something fishy going on. When the seller is selling 1000 of these products a month and selling them at such cheap prices it is impossible for this product to be legitimate, yet nothing is done to stop this. It is understandable that some people will sell their software for low prices but only once in a while, not in 1000s of units per month. Even wholesalers are unable to make these type of cuts.

EBay seems to be satisfied that this can continue, a main motivation it seems is that they yield huge profits from these fraudsters. EBay enjoy a percentage of all revenue -clearly it adds up when so many

Powersellers (sellers who are supposed to be the epitome of eBay standards) are profiting in this manner.

One other major problem with the VeRo system is that it is and continues to be open to abuse by Copyright owners themselves!!

Many copyright owners force out other legitimate eBay sellers by making VeRo complaints to eBay. EBay has a policy not to check any of these out, they are satisfied that once registered as a copyright owner you are correct in your opinion. All complaints are withdrawn from the eBay market place. I have personally been subject to several listing withdrawals by copyright owners when my product was legitimate. In my instance it was hardly worth arguing I just sold it elsewhere.

Greedy copyright holders are happy to gain a monopoly on eBay (illegal in the real business world) by forcing out other sellers.

In 2003 eBay lost a $35 million patent-infringement judgment *3, which seems to have scared them to death of incurring yet more lawsuits, so they seem to be trying to keep out of all these issues. One more recent lawsuit seems to be on track to force eBay to reconsider. In fact eBay could be hit very hard as they have a no-win situation on their hands.

As I stated earlier many copyright/trademark owners are unhappy with the huge profits being made by 'unregulated' traders on eBay and the internet generally. In the past Manufacturers and Wholesalers enjoyed the ability to pick and choose retailers who stocked their products. Today the market has become so vast one can no longer afford to monitor retailers. Tiffany Jewelers seem to be one company who are attempting to hit back.

In 2004 *4 Tiffany & Co, sued eBay Inc., claiming that eBay had aided violations of trademark by allowing counterfeit items to be sold. A Tiffany spokesman claimed that 73 per cent of Tiffany jewelry on eBay was fake which clearly affected its profits not to mention weakening its brand.

> Further more Tiffany insisted eBay either accounted for profits it made from the said counterfeit products or pay them One Million Dollars per item!

Tiffany's concern was also that eBay refused to Police the site themselves and insisted Tiffany used the VeRo program. Tiffany employed two full time employees to monitor eBay and ended 19,000 fake auctions through the VeRo program. Clearly they saw little pleasure in spending their own money on Policing eBays problem.

EBay have always responded to any trademark claim with their statement that eBay is a forum for buyers and sellers to meet not somewhere that eBay sell therefore they are not liable for the actions of others. Clearly this is starting to wear a little thin with some Trademark owners.

I'm just amazed that more people haven't mentioned that User Names or IDs often are utilised by individuals who do not own the terms.

This is a particularly interesting case because many people believe that there is far more behind Tiffany's claims than just this issue. I'm sure that eBay for instance, would settle out of court with a deal to employ several members of their own staff to monitor eBay of Tiffany products to eliminate this problem rather than just get sued. Moreover, it would be very inexpensive for eBay to set a computer program to stop all Tiffany products until monitoring had been conducted. With this accounted for, it brings up the question what is it in Tiffany's criteria that keeps them suing eBay?

One theory is that this very high profile case is scaring off illegal and legitimate resellers from selling Tiffany products hence they are benefiting massively by an increase in direct sales themselves. A knock on effect to this could reach far beyond eBay and scare off traders throughout the internet and even 'bricks and mortar' businesses.

Effectively this new tough line reputation could develop Tiffany in to a sole trader of its own products (cutting out the retailer), something that was not desirable until the advent of online trading.

EBay are clearly and rightfully scared. The ramifications are immense. If Tiffany wins it would open up the flood gates to thousands of traders and millions in court claims let alone the huge impact on eBay costs in having to start monitoring all branded and counterfeit items on their site to prevent any more legal claims. EBay would become no more! I Hope eBay are forced to re-evaluate. Other auction houses such as Christie's and Sotheby's had to check all their auctioned items for centuries at their own cost and they do not moan about it. There is no reason why eBay – who turns over more profit than the said auction houses – cannot do the same.

We will have to wait for the outcome in this case.

*1 17,000 Vero rights owner registered with eBay.co.uk – ebay.co.uk 2007
*2 all 'illegal' funds gained from researching this book were refunded to buyers, products returned or transactions cancelled on completion.
*3 2003 eBay lost a $35 million patent-infringement
*4 USA Today June 2004, http://www.usatoday.com/tech/news/2004-06-22-tiffany-ebay_x.htm

On the seller side of things you have no leg to stand on when your product apparently breaches copyright rules but in your opinion is legitimately sold. Furthermore you are not given a reason for the removal of your product. This opens up the ability for copyright owners to abuse the system as they need not give you a reason. In their own VeRo tutorial eBay states the following;

> *'Unfortunately, eBay cannot require rights owners to provide you with the exact reason for the removal of your listing. However, we do require that they provide you with an email address to contact them directly. The rights owner's email address should have been included in the email we sent to you notifying you about your listing removal.'*

eBay.co.uk - ebay VeRo tutorial - http://pages.ebay.co.uk/help/policies/questions/vero-ended-item.html

This is a problem that I have come across several times. I have been in direct competition with registered copyright owners on eBay with my own legitimate products for sale and because of my superior ability to sell and list on eBay they have become disgruntled by their own lack of ability. This is especially true if the employee doing the selling has to account to his superior as to why they are not selling as much as another trader on eBay. One easy way around this is for the employee to kick off traders who are better than they are without need for reason.

Most Traders like myself don't have the time to mess around with these people especially as we are fully aware it is likely we would get no response via their email address and eBay have deaf ears to these problems – returning an automated response of no responsibility in these matters. The following is eBays response to the above matter;

'What he should do (the removed seller -sic) is contact the rights owner. If the rights owner agrees that a mistake has been made, he or she can tell eBay, and eBay will let the trader know that it's OK to re-list his item.'

It is illegal to make and sell fake copies of CD's however, many eBayers sell them as back-up copies and get away with it. If you sell a product that you have a back-up for you are not allowed to keep the back up CDs/DVD's by law.

EBay claim that they do not allow any recordable CD's or DVD's on the site that have data on- unless you state in the description that you are the copyright owner. Again this is a policy that they do not actively police and I have seen countless items like this that have sold. The truth is you can at least double and often quadruple your product sale price by offering a back-up copy with the item if the item is in an undesirable format (such as VHS Video). You can see an example of this in Chapter Seven.

Although Trading Standards state that any copying of DVD's or CD's whether for personal use or for a friend is illegal it is wide spread.

TWO

GREAT BIG PayPal – an eBay company

What is PayPal?

PayPal has 100 million account members worldwide and is the dominating payment system on eBay. It is also owned by eBay. PayPal was acquired by eBay Inc. in October, 2002. This brings up both a number of problems and some benefits. Obviously when an online business the size of eBay regulates its own complaints system there is always a raised eyebrow or two. Whether this is a fair system is questionable and when the shop regulates both its payment system and complaints procedure then there has to be some sort of conflict of interest?

In theory, when using PayPal as a payment method on eBay traders should be protected financially. The truth is, because of eBays eagerness to settle buyer and seller disputes quickly the complaints procedure leaves much to be desired. As we will see later, during my research I discovered ways to use the PayPal system to assist traders in getting products for free and gaining an additional income from these 'free' products thereafter.

It's worth mentioning again that eBay makes money from sellers not buyers, and PayPal also make money from sellers not buyers. Even if you transfer some money to another PayPal member, PayPal will charge you a percentage of the money transferred – even if no goods or services were exchanged.

The main benefits of PayPal is its integration into eBay - obviously a main contributing factor when eBay chose to buy the company. This makes it a quick and easy way to buy and sell on eBay, moving cash quickly from various accounts or from person to person.

An issue that "newbie's" to eBay have to be aware of is that when you use both eBay to sell a product and PayPal to process the transaction essentially you are billed twice! This becomes quite costly to the traders and very financially rewarding to eBay! Many new traders fail to consider this when setting their prices on eBay and end up losing or not making the profit that they hoped for.

Setting up a PayPal account

When you join eBay you are encouraged to also open a PayPal account. In fact it is very difficult to trade on eBay without a PayPal account as around ninety percent of eBay transactions are conducted through this payment system.

In all fairness PayPal is a safe place to trade in relation to direct credit card fraud, the threat is managed relatively well. Also if you want to withdraw more than £500 per month you'll need to agree to an 'Expanded Use process'.

PayPal run a system of credit card and address confirmation upon account registration. This means that they send a letter out by mail to your home address which must coincide with the credit card that you supply. This process effectively reduces the possibility of thieves stealing credit card details and using them to buy products on eBay. Obviously, as in all fraud, there are always ways around this, but in the majority of cases it works well.

You'll need to be aware that this may create a false sense of security in new eBay users as many are blissfully unaware that this process is only conducted in the US, Canada and the UK. Other countries do not have these types of check. Slightly worrying as online fraud is rife in countries such as Asia and Africa! A lesson for the uninitiated perhaps, don't buy from anywhere except these three countries. Certainly I never purchase or sell to the Asian countries unless I can afford to lose the money or the product in question. These are countries where tracking people down is almost impossible.

> Having said all of this, in my opinion the main financial loss and pitfalls in PayPal trading emerge from a surprising place- PayPal customer services!

For instance if you are selling electronic products such as e-books or even CD's and an eBay fraudster decides to lie about receiving a product or for any other reason claim their money back, PayPal will *in almost every case* refund the buyer. This can become a costly process for the seller, not to mention the health issues from the anger it inevitably fosters.

One big negative aspect of PayPal is that you cannot withdraw money from your PayPal account into your bank account for around 7 days. This is a one sided restriction, PayPal have the ability to withdraw money immediately from your bank if they wish and you can also pay another person through instant bank withdrawal via PayPal if you desire.

This rule brings up interesting problems when trading. If a buyer makes a refund complaint, the complaint procedure takes a minimum of 10 days but you cannot make the complaint until seven days after the auction end. During the complaint procedure your funds are frozen, in other words if you rely on your eBay income to live- you are stuffed for well over two weeks!! In addition PayPal add another 10 days on to that if the complaint is upheld and you have to start the 7 day funds withdrawal process over again!

Usually if a buyer complains to you without starting the complaint procedure, you can drag the conversation out via email for a week or so in order to download your money before the account is frozen.

Often you will have a gut feeling that someone may try to claim their money back (you usually have a sixth sense for the type who will 'try it on'), transfer the funds to another account so PayPal cannot get their hands on it. You can send it to a friend or relatives account before the complaint is made. This will cost you a fee to PayPal, but it means two things *one*; you get your hands on the money you need to eat! *Two*; PayPal cannot give money back to an eBayer if there is no credit in the account. This is assuming you cut off your direct debit to PayPal, which can be done instantly if you have online banking which ensures your money is safe for now. You will have to pay at some point if you want to continue to trade using this account in the near future. If you don't mind not using your account until eBay have closed this dispute permanently you maybe able to reactivate your account without financial loss.

If you think someone will claim money back then your best bet is to transfer your money to another account so that PayPal cannot get their hands on it.

PayPal Dispute Resolution Process

There are two reasons for a dispute; 'Item significantly not as described' or 'Item not received'.

If for example a buyer claimed the item they bought from you did not arrive or as PayPal puts it 'Item Not Received', the buyer can file a dispute via PayPal, but it has to be done within 45 days of the date of the original transaction, if nothing happens or the seller is not co-operating then the buyer can escalate the dispute into a claim but no later than 20 days from the date your dispute was filed. If the dispute is not escalated to a claim within 20 days the dispute will automatically close.

Like most eBay company policies – it's getting complicated!

So if someone files a dispute against you and 19 days after filing the dispute they escalate it to a claim. PayPal say they will make every effort to resolve the matter within 30 days. So in all that can amount to 50 days for a seller to have his income frozen, in some instances for no good reason. You can see how much pressure is on the buyer to give in – virtually blackmailed in some cases. Remember that the seller who's account is frozen is not allowed to buy or sell with this account, if they also source their products on eBay it could put them out of business for months.

The payment dispute timeframe can be of great assistance to the "Hustler", especially if trading abroad.

Verification

When you open a PayPal account it is automatically restricted to no more than £500 worth of withdrawals per month for three months or an overall limit of £1500. This is a security measure, so if a Hustler is going to con people with a new account he can do so with a limit of £1500 per fake account – still not a bad profit for a con artist!

To lift this limit you will need to verify a bank account or add a credit card. This process essentially confirms either that you live at the given address or you have access to the said bank account. As mentioned before this process is currently only available to USA, Canadian and UK users, other countries do not run verification programs – something to think about when trading abroad!

Buyer Protection

PayPal offer 'Buyer Protection' and claim to enhance a buyers confidence with this service. The service was born out of huge media and buyer dissatisfaction in the way sellers could send faulty items with no repercussions. PayPal had to be seen doing something and this protection became the solution. Consequently the service is bordering on being a mere gimmick, in reality it does not do the job it claims to do.

Firstly PayPal do not offer this to all sellers. You are required to have a trading history long enough for PayPal to have made at least some cash out of you. This means to qualify you need to have a rating of 98 percent and above with feedback of at least 50.

This service is often mistaken for Insurance, which it is not. Remember, we stated earlier that eBay seems to favour the seller as they are the money generating machine. With PayPal 'Buyer Protection Claims' it's my experience that they almost always favour the buyer and refund the traders money. Hence the Seller loses out- both on a product, the postage cost which will be lost and the money which needs to be refunded.

This service has become a great way for the fraudster to make cash. It often does the opposite to what PayPal claim it does. Instead of protecting people and perhaps helping to insure buyers, it encourages buyers to refuse purchasing insurance. Why would a buyer spend extra money on insurance and increasing the cost of their purchases, when they can claim money back for free, leaving the claim costs to be paid by the seller, and almost always winning not only the cost of the product back, but to retain the product as well! In most cases the buyer will be quite wound up by the time of a refund that they do not send the product back and PayPal will not monitor this.

PayPal insist that the buyer sends the item back to the seller when a refund has been given however, in reality you will find few buyers sending the product back and in some cases even reselling it on eBay! There is no reason in my opinion that PayPal could not insist on products which have had refunds to be sent to a PayPal official to forward to the seller to ensure that the transaction took place.

Even if the seller of an item insists on postage insurance from a third party to be taken out for his auctions PayPal don't care, unless sellers can prove tracking. Receipts of payment etc are not sufficient under their rules. (This is the opposite stance to eBays view who will not ever refund damaged or lost items in transit unless insurance is taken out.)

If the seller takes out insurance with the postal service they are protected by any damage or loss of an item but the obvious problem arises, this will raise selling costs dramatically if listing multiple items. To most high volume traders this is simply not feasible.

Another problem arises from these cases where insurance has been taken out and the seller claims money back from the postal service and refunds the buyer himself. The problem here is that if the buyer decides to go ahead with the PayPal claim even though they have already been refunded by the seller they may get their money back twice!

> So if you are a seller trying to avoid claim backs for broken/lost or damaged goods continue to sell to new accounts that have feedback of less than 50 and with poor ratings of under 98 % this way they cannot make a claim through PayPal!

If you think PayPal protection is a rip off you should check out eBays standard purchase protection programme! It only gives you partial reimbursement for losses resulting from non-delivery or misrepresentation of most items up to £120 GBP and they have the nerve to charge YOU a £15 processing cost – outrageous! This has to be seen as an incentive not to make a claim?

THREE

GREAT BIG eBay Rules and how to get around them!

To keep relatively media friendly eBay have been keen to be seen tackling the fraud issue with anti-fraud software and employing ex-White House security staff to advise on cyber issues. Although serious fraud is something that the Police are responsible for, it seems eBay keep some 'illegal' activity from the general public by dismissing the true extent of fraud thus avoiding adverse media coverage.

The true facts are that total reported losses (it is assumed many more frauds are not reported) filed to the FBI Internet fraud squad were as follows;[1] $17 million in 2002, $54 million in 2003, $64 million in 2004 and $183 million in 2005 and so on.

It is also clear that the easily dealt with minor issues such as Shill Bidding could be totally eliminated with software if eBay so wished. We can only assume there is financial gain to be made by not sorting these problems. Having said this I'm not entirely sure why eBay mark shill bidding as an illegal activity because this is the whole essence of auction trading. In fact you can do little else but bid at the last minute at "bricks and mortar auctions" which have been in existence for decades.

There are several forms of 'fraud' that are not allowed on eBay. Some of these are not [2] lawfully illegal but eBay rules and are in reality extensively used by traders to gain higher profits from their sales. These techniques are also often used in a more sinister way to sabotage other seller's auctions. Either in order to gain advantage for their own products or to force out the competition. Sometime it's just a malicious activity.

EBay even rates some of these activities as serious or not so. Seems strange to have rules then dilute their seriousness by rating the level of naughtiness - almost saying some activities are OK? And of course, we've seen that different 'levels' of trader are allowed to 'get away with' a varying amount of rule breaking depending on their 'status', as seen in chapter one the 'Powerseller marketplace compliance policy'.

> As eBay doesn't regulate this behaviour adequately, some traders might feel it is worth considering using these techniques for their own gains. In fact, you may have problems making a profit on eBay without these as they will be used against you by other sellers, and you must use these to survive. It's dog eat dog on eBay.

The main victim as we will see later, is the uninitiated on eBay or 'new' users that most often become drawn into to these scams and pay over the odds for your product.

EBay have been keen to 'look as if' they have enhanced their security measures but have done little to stop the everyday manipulation of experienced traders that makes eBay such a minefield to the uninitiated.

EBay have integrated their own anti-fraud software that claims to 'flag-up' potential fraud. From case studies set out later you'll notice that even when perpetrators are discovered next to nothing is done. In fact eBay often leave the dirty work to the Law enforcement services that inevitably take months to develop a good enough case for court, when eBay could have just nipped it in the bud from the beginning or even better prevented it with software. It seems odd that eBay encourages traders to communicate and solve their own problems when they seem unwilling to stop even the most evident cases of fraud. I have in this book outlined emails returned from eBay following a submission by myself upon noticing stolen property listed. I was directed to basically 'sort it out myself'! I was directed to a form on eBay where I should inform a Police Officer and get them to fill out the form. EBay would then consider the issue! As if a local copper would bother filling an online form out for eBay! Not to mention the fact that I was not going to go out of my way if eBay could not be bothered!

One motivational factor for eBay to allow fraud to continue is the statistic that under their own admission;

> "Overall, fraud on eBay occurs in less than 0.01 percent of its listings, Typically, 16 million items are listed for sale daily on eBay." - eBay spokesman Kevin Pursglove.

Naught point naught one percent sounds Ok doesn't it? Well, when you put that in statistic into perspective, out of 16 million items listed, it works out at 1600 frauds per day or 112,000 per week!!! Not so respectable huh, eBay?

1* http://www.fbi.gov/pressrel/pressrel06/internetcrimereport.htm To obtain a copy of IC3's 2005 Internet Crime Report, visit; www.ic3.gov/media/annualreports.aspx

*2 please note law varies from country to country and state to state some of these techniques may have custodial sentences attached to their actions. The law in your jurisdiction must be considered when considering partaking in eBay techniques.

Black Market goods

In other words counterfeit products or 'fake' copies. Most often these goods are CD's, DVD's and videos, basically products that can be easily copied with a home computer. With so many electrical goods on the market today and the ease at which one can transfer this data across the internet, it is of little surprise that illegal copies of these products are available on eBay in vast quantities.

Counterfeiting is growing rapidly and is said to account for seven percent of Gross Domestic Product (the market value of goods and services produced within a country).

The main way to distinguish a fake product on eBay is if it hasn't got a picture in its listing and if the seller claims it comes with no packaging. It's understandable if the seller does not have its original receipt or outer packaging as we rarely retain these. However, if it's a CD there should be a jewel case or cover/sleeve. Most home copiers are still unable to reproduce perfect sleeves, although this is not always the case.

EBay will claim that selling counterfeit products is prohibited but it does little to quash the trend. The fact is that if a trader is not listed with a business account and can't prove that they have a wholesale/ trade account with a manufacturer, but they continue to sell multiple items of the same product, it is likely that these are counterfeit.

> In fact in nearly every case of traders researched for this book who have been imprisoned for counterfeiting on eBay, they had previously been suspended (sometimes more than once) by eBay but continue to trade successfully.

EBay does have a policy to suspend a traders account if violations are continually ignored but as we will see later, it is only when another trader makes a complaint about your product that eBay become aware and usually this person has to be a member of their 'community'. EBay does not monitor feedback, only complaints, although the new system bought out in 2007 may change this. If you keep customer satisfaction (not feedback) high you can continue to trade and avoid this. In the case study later you will see that traders are making thousands of pounds duplicating pirated CD's on a monthly basis without repercussions.

It has to be noted that the selling of counterfeit reproductions is against the law and trading standards can prosecute guilty parties. It also should be noted that only those who reproduce in vast quantities and continue to ignore legal warnings ever get prosecuted. The cost of court action and the negative Public Relations are too high.

In these cases suspension of your eBay account usually occurs before any legal proceeding – which is easily rectified with the opening of a new account. In fact in nearly every case of traders researched for this book who have been imprisoned for counterfeiting on eBay, they had previously been suspended by eBay but continued to trade successfully.

Defective goods

This is simply advertising goods as in working order when in fact they are defective. There are various degrees of fault and exaggeration of condition. Some people just fail to note damage which, in theory, is not necessarily done to deceive but in eBay terms still not being honest.

EBay do make the ambiguous statement that the product has to be **'significantly not as described'** in comparison to the products listing description in their criteria for a complaint. If your product has some damage then it is always a good idea to take a photo and put this in the description this way if a buyer claims their money back they will not get it.

Not mentioning an items poor condition is simply more aggravation than it is worth. The buyer will simply file a complaint and will usually get a refund and in many cases you will be left both out of pocket and without your product being returned. If you really want to shift a dodgy product and are happy to lie through your teeth as many eBayers are, you can sell the product and when the buyer complains you make a complaint that they switched products as you sent a perfect item. See switching product scam and Misrepresentation later on in this book.

Fee stacking

Adding hidden charges to an item once the auction has ended. This is quite difficult as eBay has tightened up the ability to change listings once a buyer has made the first bid. Techniques to blind customers are easier to accomplish.

Psychologically you will gain more money if you set your postage rate higher than the actual postal cost as people get stuck in the moment of bidding and don't focus too much on the postal rate. This is a useful trap when first time bidders start to trade on eBay as they are usually blissfully unaware of multiple postal charges on one single product. EBay have recently begun to add postal rates next to the item cost to enhance buyers awareness of the added costs. Even so, bidders will still get caught in the moment and ignore a higher than normal postage cost. On eBay very few people list postage exactly as it will cost.

One reason is that buyers rarely take into account postage. Even when they do they will pay more for a product if some of the profit is added to the postage – see the next chapter on psychological ways of winning. The second reason postage will be higher than actual cost is that sellers do need to take into account packaging and storage costs as well, just incase the item sells at a low price.

If you are selling to international clients it is easy to add several levels of postage for different countries and once the item has been won, add more postage than the wining bidder anticipated, and much more than it will actually cost to send. You could for instance claim to send the parcel to America by airmail but actually send it by sea, which is much slower and less expensive. Not the best technique for maintaining good relations with your customers!

In 2007 eBay initiated a new 'star' rating system that allows buyers to leave additional feedback about a sellers postage rates, this is intended to encourage sellers to give honest postal costs. This is not good for sellers as profit margins are bound to fall – but we will see.

Misrepresentation

This is unacceptable in eBay terms however there are subtle ways to achieve this trick whilst being 'honest' and staying within the rules.

EBay does not allow deliberate deceit. Whether it's a false description, picture of a different product (unless stated in the description) or deception to the value of an item. It is perfectly Ok to use other listings to create the assumption in the market place of product values. For instance, if you have several 'watchers' (buyers who have flagged your product to purchase later) in your auction but the price is not as high as would like. You might like to open a new eBay account or to get a friend (preferably in a different city although you can alter your second account to suggest a different location) to add a separate listing that will finish after yours. You'll need to list a similar product but bid it up or set a high 'buy it now' price to create the perception that your product is worth a great deal more than it actually is. Once your product has been bid up high and sold you can end the fake listing. This can work but you need to be careful, as too many similar products ending closely together have an effect of reducing the winning price of your listing. So to ensure success you need to make sure there are only a few similar products and their price is high. This is not strictly misrepresentation, but you are deliberately insinuating a higher value/demand for your product – again arguably against eBay rules.

Many people accidentally misrepresent products that they perceive as being worth more than they actually are. You cannot be blamed for lack of buyer knowledge if a trader buys your product thinking it is something that it's not- as long as you are (perceived to be) honest in your listing. One area that this is a concern is the area of collectables. Manufacturers swap and change product colours and change manufacturing techniques or models constantly. For this reason collectable items may seem to be the same but a small distinguishing feature may, to the expert, tell it apart from its cheaper twin.

If a trader has done their homework they can often list a less expensive look-a-like next to a more expensive product (or even better put a link to a sold item in their description) to convince buyers that their item is worth a great deal more.

They can of course claim innocence when the buyer discovers

that they bought the wrong item. They were honest –to their knowledge, in the description no-one will blame them. Lesson learned for the buyer. This is why asking specific questions on an item is essential to potential buyers.

One similar technique that is often used successfully is to list an item with a picture of two DVD cases (rather than one) of separate products but actually list one DVD for sale in the description. This is not Misrepresentation as such because the seller is telling the truth, the problem lies in peoples need for speed and buyers not bothering to read the body text correctly. Thanks to this governments policies this is becoming easier and easier as the young poorly educated generation are coming of age. Easily duped by their poor reading and writing skills they are turned into easy victims.

In the description it is made clear that the sale is for one item only. Buyers often skip through listings with large amounts of text and fail to realise that the auction is for one not two DVD's. They then go ahead and pay over the odds for the product. Buyers often feel foolish when they complain following close inspection of the listing and actually end up apologising for their behaviour and giving the seller good feedback. After all, the seller was perfectly honest in their listing and it was the buyers mistake. EBay will back the seller up in that there is no ground for complaint.

It should be noted that Consumer Protection from Unfair Trading Regulations were implemented on 26 May 2008. This could see unfair practices becoming criminal offences, how these acts will be proved as being deliberate is another matter!

Although the above picture shows two CD cases, the item will be listed as one CD sale and clearly marked as such in the listing description. Many people will assume without reading the description that two CD's are on offer, hence pay a higher price.

Multiple self bidding (see also shill bidding)

There are many ways of enhancing your listing and profits by using more than one User ID. Although eBay forbids you using multiple ID's to bid on an item, technology wise they still allow it to happen. The technology is available to stop this practice but they clearly choose not to. Perhaps because an increase in the sale price of an item increases their commission?

One way to increase profits in this way is to place multiple bids using different ID's. By placing a ridiculously high price on somebody else's product you effectively drive out other potential buyers. When you get close to the auction end you withdraw your high bid and the price plummets to its former lower bid that you also placed with another ID. Hopefully due to the former high price no-one is watching this item and you win the product at a low price.

EBay have tried to stop this practice, but their efforts are somewhat weak. They have introduced a scheme where if you bid before the final 12 hours of an items ending time and you retract your bid, all your bids using ALL of your ID's are cancelled. But you can not retract bids during the last 12 hours if you placed them before the final 12 hours.

If you bid during the last 12 hours of an item ending you can only retract within an hour of placing that bid – *have you got that*!

Although these rules are in place, you can easily contact a seller and ask them to withdraw a bid at anytime, they will often do so to keep in good faith with other eBayers. If you come up with a good enough excuse for bidding them up they should go for it. Remember, they will be unaware that you have multiple ID's and are the owner of a similar auction.

Another Multiple Bid tactic often seen is to bid on an item that ends after your product ends. When similar items end close to each other they normally reduce the ending sale price of the first. To avoid another trader selling a similar product after your item ends and reducing your product price you might bid using a different ID on the competitions product so that it sells for more than yours. Potential buyers then perceive that yours is both better value and worth more than you anticipated. Hence they start to bid on your product. As soon as your auction ends you retract your bid from the other auction. Job done.

Because eBay only bids up in increments (proxy biding) (i.e. if you bid £100 on an item that currently costs 99p it will put a proportion of your £100 bid above 99 pence until another bidder bids) you will need to have multiple ID's to first bid the 99 pence and then to bid up to the £100 mark for multiple bid tactics to be effective.

Again retracting bids in this way is officially 'not allowed' by eBay but is possible and rife on the eBay market place.

Non-delivery

A self explanatory term, you buy an item, but you never receive the goods. Often when this happens you will also receive no response from the seller and most often this is a private seller rather than a registered business. EBay almost always gives your money back in these cases. Obviously there are occasions that a seller will say that an item has been dispatched, but in actual fact the item never actually existed. Again eBay almost always refunds money, which does as we'll see later, open up opportunities for some serious abuse and fraud.

> Incidentally this is the most complained about fraudulent activity associated with online auction sites. *1

EBay seems only to settle with sellers if they paid for tracking on the item such as 'Recorded Delivery'. An unlikely event in that costs start to increase.

Non-payment

Due to the nature of eBay this is a very rare occurrence. The buyer receives the goods, but refuses to pay. As the majority of transactions are conducted through PayPal instant payment or at least payment before posting the product is the norm it is a difficult scam to execute. This is most likely to occur when a cheque or echeque is sent and the seller inadvertently or out of good faith sends the product before cheques are cleared or received. Sending products before payment is to be avoided at all costs and good faith is a luxury eBayers do not offer! From my experience eBay users are very crafty and have very low moral standards and as the younger generation start using this site their standards are being desensitised by fraud and it is becoming more and more acceptable.

> Sending products before payment is to be avoided at all costs and good faith is a luxury eBayers do not offer!

As in many of the techniques researched for this book, when non payment occurs it is the Seller rather than the Buyer who suffers.

EBay have now bought in the option to receive instant payment when you list an item as a 'Buy–it now' listing. What this has done is remove the possibility of non-payment within these types of auctions as long as PayPal is used as the payment system. With this option the item remains for sale even if a trader has purchased it and remains for sale until the buyer sends money. This eliminates buyers from ruining your listing by bidding but not paying. Obviously this has cut down the instances of complaints to eBay of non payment.

Shield bidding

This is exactly the same technique as multiple self bidding with more than one ID except the bidder allows a friend to also bid against them and retract their high bid at the last minute. Again the first bidder ends up winning the auction at a low price. Although forbidden by eBay again it is possible and happens frequently. This is much harder to detect by eBay as they cannot know who your friends are.

This was done to me when I was selling my car. An eBayer bid on the car and dropped out later on. Although it was not at the last minute as eBay have stopped you from doing this, it was long enough for most of the potential buyers who visited my site to lose interest and ruin my auction. Later upon more detailed investigation I found the trader who dropped out of my auction had a similar car on eBay selling after my car. The high price he'd bid on my car (which was a much better buy than his) discouraged buyers from buying mine and encouraged buyers to bid on his lower priced car. It worked, by the time I realised what was going on his car was sold and mine was not.

Remember that your number of bid retractions is displayed in your member profile for all to see however, nobody really checks these when they buy from you. But with too many of these you are heading for an eBay suspension.

Shill bidding

This is the intentional bidding up ones own auction either using an alternative ID as in multiple self bidding or asking a friend to do the dirty work. Or increasing the apparent desirability of your item. This is classed as very serious in eBays world and you can have your Powerseller status withdrawn for such a dastardly act!

> It is interesting to note that eBay themselves were taken to court for Shill bidding and lost the case. We will discuss this further later.

Again although forbidden by eBay it is a practice very hard to regulate unless eBay chooses to stop traders having multiple ID's, or to stop traders being able to bid on their own ID's which is very easy to prevent if they chose to.

EBay has set up the software to prevent traders from bidding on their own main account but if they open another they can bid on that account. Obviously if eBay can prevent the activity on one account they can do it on all accounts.

It's almost as if eBay encourage users to shill bid, one reason I say this is because everyone is doing it. Later in this chapter you will see how, for research purposes, I deliberately shill bid my own auctions without reprisal. Eventually, my account was suspended on a temporary basis, and it was other peoples involvement that caused this not my own activity.

It's true to say that as long as shill bidding is allowed to continue eBay make more money because they take a greater commission if a product sells for a higher price. Not to mention the fact that the more profit traders make the more likely it is that they will trade more products on eBay.

It is interesting to note that if eBay claim that they do not encourage Shill bidding, I am curious to know why they allow a trader to open a new ID and list the ID's location elsewhere to the account location, even if the account's use is on the same computer IP address? The only reason for traders to do this is to fool buyers in believing the two ID's are not related and thus enabling stealth shill bidding.

I appreciate that some large volume sellers have other members of staff working for them so prefer to have them use separate ID's. I would argue that this is a minority and the problem of shill biding out weighs the benefit of the odd trader wanting multiple ID's for staff.

> FBI investigations into shill biding and eBay buyer rings found that these scams were rife! Using the same data that eBay used in their investigations and subsequently found no evidence of fraud, the FBI managed to bring charges and convictions. *3

This is illegal in some States of America and also in Britain, but I have not come across anyone who has been investigated by law agencies in England, if they were many eBayers would begin to worry!

Switching goods

This technique has been used since eBay started and continues today. Often hard to prove and both eBay and PayPal rarely settle these matters on side of the seller- who loses out in this case.

In this situation a seller sells a perfectly good item, usually high end, a computer accessory or digital camera for example. The winning buyer waits for the arrival of the new/ good condition item and swaps it with a broken model of the same spec that he already has in his possession. The buyer then returns the product as broken or defective in some way claiming it was already broken or broken in transit. The buyer then receives a full refund from PayPal plus he now has replaced his old defective product with a new working model.

Some sellers don't even realise this fraud has occurred and actually believe their item was damaged in transit. One possible sign is that most broken items have a considerable amount of wear and tear in comparison to items that are in good working order.

As an attempt at a solution some sellers choose to mark their products with infrared signatures or codes to check whether they have returned the correct item. Even so if the buyer chooses not to accept their attempt at fraud PayPal will still in most cases side with the buyer (fraudster).

Credit Card fraud

This is extremely unlawful and can end you up in prison fairly quickly. Usually conducted by the hardened criminal and too sophisticated for the normal eBayer and certainly not within the realms of a law abiding citizen.

If you are a victim in most cases your credit card company will refund you the amount lost. You will need to supply all documentation and eBay/PayPal info for a proper investigation. Also credit card companies usually require a crime number from your police station. This is issued when you report a crime. Credit card companies (unlike PayPal) always support their customers' product and financial losses.

In eBays defence, this sort of crime has been reduced dramatically and it's very hard to instigate on eBay if using a PayPal account. With their introduction of address confirmation for PayPal accounts it's difficult to open an account, receive payments or download payments without leaving a trail. Of course PayPal accounts can be hacked into but again the money still needs to be converted from electronic to hard cash for the fraudster to complete the crime for personal gain.

This is one problem listing a current account rather than a credit card (which PayPal encourages) with your PayPal account because if your PayPal account is accessed the crook can withdraw all your money from your current account. With a credit card there is a limit and most credit card companies will re-reimburse fraudulent transactions.

Although it's an unfortunate fact that online fraud with credit cards is to some extent unavoidable if your credit card has been stolen in most case the credit card companies will reimburse your cash.

One useful advent of the internet is the new ability to access online bank accounts instantly. Therefore, if you suspect any unusual behaviour you can quite often check your account relatively quickly.

It might be worth noting that *4 The National Consumers League found that the majority of reported frauds in online auctions paid with either a cheque (32%), or a money order (48%). Credit cards were low on the list.

Stolen goods

Obviously the sale of stolen goods knowingly or otherwise is illegal and to be avoided. As stated earlier I personally made eBay aware of what I was advised was a piece of stolen property on eBay and they seemed totally unconcerned. They merely sent me an email stating I should contact the Police myself and ask them to fill out an online form! It seems eBay feel they can police themselves! The said product was not taken off eBay even though the description stated that it may be stolen.

There are many products that lend themselves to the stolen market. These are high value desirable products such as mobile phones. It is quite easy to dramatically reduce this problem if buyers insist on receipts of purchase, sight of contracts or even to ensure the phone has a box. Mobile phones are unlike many other products in that most mobile phone owners retain their boxes, contracts etc.

Other violations

In line with eBays perceived policy of prejudice between various types of eBay Trader, eBay has set out specific rules identifying what you are not allowed to do. These are open to interpretation especially if you are a favoured member such as a Powerseller.

EBay considers the following activities as "Severe policies":

- Shill Bidding
- Misrepresentation of Identity
- Site Interference
- Transaction Interference
- User agreement violations

EBay consider the following activities as not allowed. But they are not considered 'serious' under their rules, make of that as you will!

Keyword spamming – I have always done this and it works very well. The key to stop other traders being aware of this is to make the spamming key words as small as possible and the same colour as the background. You'll not get complaints this way. Most people don't search descriptions so this is limited in effectiveness unless the item is rare.

Links Policy – This using links such as hyper links to other websites, pages or email accounts. You won't be taken off if you link to your own site unless somebody tells eBay. This is not considered very serious and the most likely event is that you are told to remove the listing. Suspension can occur and eBay claim they can remove the listing and keep your fee.

Misleading Titles – Most eBayers list titles that will get them the most traffic and this is practiced by most eBayers. Again, keyword spamming is essential – see later example.

Payment Surcharges – All charges must be built into the listing price without charging extra for paying by cheque for example.

Spam - If you spam to get more customers to use your eBay email addresses, do it off eBay that way you are not violating the rules. Spamming is difficult on eBay because you need to type a password in when you send emails internally, this said I still get spam through my eBay account frequently.

Categorisation of Listing - Items must be listed in the 'correct' category. Breaches of this policy may result in punishment! This is a ridiculous rule, categories to a large degree are seller 'dependant' it can amount to the sellers perception. There are a lot of items that could fit in multiple sections of eBay.

Categories also vary from country to country – for example you can not list in the category 'Triathlon' in England but America has this category.

Source;*http://pages.ebay.co.uk/services/buyandsell/powerseller/criteria.html*

How to avoid it

Avoiding General Online Auction Fraud

- Study how the Auction website works before buying or selling. A quick search on a search engine can give you an idea of the problems other traders have experienced.
- Consider how the complaints procedure is conducted by the website.
- Consider taking third party insurance if necessary particularly on

shipping.
- Research the buyer if selling an item. Often a quick domain search can reveal the traders home or business address, if so do they match the details of the auction site? Also Companies House is easily accessed for company details if the trader claims to be a business.
- Consider feedback and check it is not just a buying account.
- Consider if the buyer / seller is located in a country other than the ones protected by eBay and PayPal.

Avoiding Non-Delivery of Merchandise

- Research the seller of a product to ensure they are honest.
- Research any bad feedback or withdrawn feedback. If there is any evidence of non-delivery avoid this seller.
- Be cautious when dealing with individuals from outside your own country, don't trade with Asian and African counties unless you can risk losing the money. Buy from Thailand for instance, and lose your money you will have very little comeback.
- Find out about returns policy's.
- Most credit card companies will give you your money back if fraud is evident in an auction, so contrary to popular belief using a credit card is one of the safest methods of payment.
- Use a prepaid credit card to avoid excessive loses if the details are stolen.

[1] The Internet Crime Complaint Center (IC3), - www.ic3.gov - Non-delivery of merchandise and non-payment accounted for 16% of complaints. "Internet auction fraud was by far the most reported offense, comprising 62.7% of referred complaints."

[2] www.ebaysucks.com/news.shtml - February 11th 2002.

[3] - http://www.fbi.gov/majcases/fraud/internetschemes.htm

[4] E-Commerce and Internet Auction Fraud: The E-Bay Community Model. Date: April 29, 2004 Source: Computer Crime Research Center, By: MOHAMED S. WAHAB

FOUR

The GREAT BIG eBay Search Engine

How to secretly use eBays marketing machine

As eBay grows many traders are realising that eBay is essentially a great big search engine. In fact, there are many benefits in viewing eBay as a search engine rather than an online shop.

AO- Auction Optimisation

Auction Optimisation (AO) is a relatively new term to describe the activity of tweaking ones listing to gain as much traffic as possible. The term was born from its sister technology Search Engine Optimisation (SEO) often used on personal websites to gain search engine ranking in order to gain traffic.

What many people do not know is that by optimising your eBay listings you can be optimising your search engine listings simultaneously. This can be very profitable.

The main way to optimise a listing is to add specific high traffic keywords to your items titles; cynics would call this keyword spamming. Although the rules set out by eBay forbid key word spamming it is virtually impossible to make serious amounts of money on eBay without using creative keywords in the titles of your listing. With careful consideration often you can do this whilst keeping within the official guidelines.

Let me give you an example, when a sad and lonely trader reported me to eBay for keyword spamming and subsequently got my listing removed.

    I was listing a highly popular sports CD called 'Archery Excellence' which was, as its name suggests an Archery Improvement Hypnosis CD.

As you might imagine there are very few potential customers who actively search 'Archery Hypnosis' as a term in itself either on eBay or in search engines. What this means is that I am unlikely to sell any CD's if I don't attract buyers by other means. Or as in this case, put my listing in a popular category in front of archers looking for something else.

    So as always I listed my CD in Bows and Arrows section with the following title;

'Archery Excellence – proven results Bows and Arrows'.

    Some trader with more time on his hands than cells in his head made a complaint to eBay and had my listing removed as it does indeed, contravene eBay rules of keyword spamming. What the trader hadn't banked upon was my superior knowledge. Within minutes I had my listing back up and running and within the guidelines.

    You see, if you make a sentence with your keywords the listing is allowed. Granted, this is often difficult with the restricted number of characters allowed in titles but it can be done.

The following title was uploaded.

'Archery EXCELLENCE – Proven! Use with Bows and Arrows.'

You'll see that the high traffic key words 'Bows and Arrows' remained, but I was using them as an advert in a sentence. Which meant I still received the traffic I wanted both from the keyword 'Archery', and Bows and Arrows.

Here is another example for the same product but using the Keywords 'Target' and 'Archery';

'Archery EXCELLENCE – Proven! Hit Targets Automatically'

> Incidentally, if I did not use keyword spamming I would usually get around 150 to 200 hits in a 10 day listing for the Archery CD's. With keyword spamming I would receive around 1000 hits per 10 day listing. That is more hits than some external websites get in a month. And that's just one title. So you can see the benefit in getting this right.

We will see in the next section that careful keyword selection not only gets you thousands of eBay hits but will help you in other search engines.

Optimising eBay for Google!

Google and eBays cosy little partnership helps them both financially. But we are concerned about making money for ourselves not what's good for them.

This means getting your own website more hits both by using eBay marketing and Google simultaneously.

The main point here is to make sure your listing in eBay has the correct keywords for a good Google placement and then make sure that when a customer clicks on the Google ad they not only go to your eBay listing but then move on to your own website hence you get a sale without paying eBay fees.

We've already said that by paying for a *'Featured Plus*!' listing on eBay gets you a good first page listing on Google, but many of you will be dubious about this due to the additional cost. At the time of writing it costs an extra £9.95 per listing in the featured section. Even so two points should be remembered here;

One, it will cost you £9.95 extra however, an advert on Google in a high traffic market can easily cost you £30 to £50 per day and you are competing with other advertisers. Not to mention the fact that paid adverts get fewer hits than natural listings which an eBay listing will come under.

Two; If you make sure your listing lasts the maximum amount of days (10) you will get top exposure and cost effectiveness. You must either list more than one product (which you can do for the same price of £9.95) so the listing remains listed for the full term or increase your product profit margin. If your listing is 'Buy it now' you could get a sale in one day and lose the extra 9 days of exposure. If your product sells with a profit of less than £9.95 you are losing money.

Driving traffic to your own commercial website

As we have already said it is against eBay rules to drive traffic to your own commercial website from eBay but this is a grey area. And in all honesty eBay do turn a blind eye to this unless one of the many eBay nerds make a complaint about your listing you should carry on without problems. Here are some ways that you can drive eBay traffic to your own website and in doing so save fees.

User Names

Make your user name your website address. I have been using my website address in some form as my 'User ID' for several years and even communicated with numerous eBay staff quoting the name without any problems. What I mean by this ID format is as follows. My eBay user ID is SportsHypnosis_co_uk and my website domain name is www.SportsHypnosis.co.uk. Now anyone who knows anything about websites will know that the underscore in my User ID is meant to represent the dot in co dot uk, but one is currently not allowed to use dots on eBay ID's. Although this seems to be set to change as eBay realise the potential of building a search engine.

If you have a products on eBay users will also have a look at your website for more products and /or information. An excellent way to get an eBay trader to visit your site is to list an item with a small amount of information in the description and state that for more information visit the following site and list your site.

Domain name placements

Adding your domain in feedback comments is allowed on eBay – actually there is no rule for this so in theory you can't be criticised.

Hundreds of people check out a traders feedback comments before buying or bidding on an item. Therefore if you leave positive feedback for a trader make a small comment and then leave your full private website address. This not only gets traders to your site, but the visitors are likely to be people looking for your type of product. Remember this will only work well if you have a descriptive domain name so traders become interested in or at least curious in what you sell. Even traders on the 'Low IQ Society' can't be mistaken by the type of business I'm in by my domain name.

Example feedback;

Thanks – Fast payment- Great eBayer.   www.SportsHypnosis.co.uk

You also should be aware that Google placements are very much down to 'link popularity' and the more places that you put an external link to your website (such as this) the better. The next placement will also assist you in this way.

The other way to place your website address in listings is to add it to your banner image in your shop. My banner image always showcases my website address at the bottom of the banner so potential customers can go to my real website should they wish.

Placing penny bids

It is not unusual for traders to 'checkout' the competition when considering bidding upon a product. This means seeing who has already bid. So this becomes an excellent form of exposure for your website. Especially if you only bid on specific market places that attract buyers who will be interested in your website. To use my example again Sports Hypnosis clients are likely to be people who are looking at all types of sports equipment and services. Therefore, I will place penny bids upon all types of equipment from Clay Pigeon clothing to Footballs.

This technique is only useful as a marketing idea if you only bid on penny items with very low or free postage costs. You don't want to end up paying hundreds of pounds out and only sell a few £5 products yourself. Most penny auctions go for more than a penny so you should be safe in most instances. If you do win an item a penny won't break the bank and you can always sell it on for a profit if you need to – watch out for high postage cost's though!

I often place bids for £100,000 Ferraris! Not with an intention in buying them because I only bid when they are selling for a few thousand pounds and the seller is not going to let me have it at that price. If I do win one day I'd be more than happy to buy and resell the car for a profit. So it is risk free and give good exposure. Having said this eBays new system of hiding all bidders ID's until they have won the auction is putting a stop to this practice for the short term. But my prediction is that eBay will have to bring the exposed ID system back because hiding ID's is leaving eBay open to much further abuse from shill bidding etc.

About me page

Officially eBay allows you to link your 'about me' page to your own commercial website. The rules state that this is the only place on eBay where you can legitimately place a commercial website link – (in reality this is not actually true) but if you want to stay within the rules this is how you do it.

More recently eBay have developed a new section called 'services' in the form of 'classified ads' which promotes local services such as website design etc. A move that is likely to turn eBay into a pure search engine rather than auction site and consequently in my opinion weaken their brand as an auction site. However, we can make use of this as they are allowing promotion of website in this section too. So if you can think of a way that you can promote your product as a service you may be able to list and link. In America where these ads have been around for a while, the word is that they generate much more traffic and sales. This is probably because if you list a service traders tend to believe that you are genuine and not a fraud, which can be the case in the original listing style auction formats.

FIVE

GREAT BIG psychological ways of winning.

Why people pay more on eBay than a product is worth!

We're all aware of the adrenaline rush one gets from gambling. Some would be surprised at the rush of adrenaline experienced by an auction style site.

This is one key to eBays success. Sellers and buyers become addicted to the fight of an auction style battle, the rush of excitement or disappointment of winning or losing. The highs and lows.

The reason this works is because buyers get caught in the moment and bid higher than expected. Time limits of an auction can only enhance this panic behaviour.

Panic buying

One phenomenon of the eBay era is the advent of many products that sell well above the normal retail price or the products true value. The same is also true of many products that sell below their retail value. In fact I will discuss later a system where you can take advantage of 'Power Sellers' who need to shift products to keep their status on eBay at prices well below their true value.

One technique many hardened eBayers utilise is to use other online websites and 'bricks and mortar' discount shops to source cut price products. Strangely, once a buyer finds the product they are after on eBay they often fail to check elsewhere, the products true value. One excellent way to use this technique is to source products from Amazon bookstore and re-sell at an auction style eBay sale.

I saw excellent profits when I decided to source a product from Amazon in order to research this book. It was during the Christmas and New Year period where I anticipated an increase in Yoga DVD sales due to an influx of celebrities bringing out such products. Celebrity endorsements often have an effect of creating consumer awareness of the whole industry, not just the specific product being offered.

I decided to source a product from a well known celebrity. I chose Geri Halliwell as she'd bought out several such DVD's in the past which meant I might be able to buy a cut price 'older' version which would add to my profit margin.

Another profit making aspect of buying from online stores is that they often offer discount postage if multiple items are ordered simultaneously. This is the case with Amazon, so I knew that I could bulk buy from Amazon with low postage costs and then split the products to sell separately and add postage to each auction thus gaining additional profit.

I was buying these Geri DVD's for £2.53 on Amazon.co.uk. Because I bought more than seven copies at one time I qualified for free postage from Amazon as I'd ordered more than £15 worth of products. I could then add postage to my eBay listing to help gain some extra profit. EBayers were buying these at around £15.00 each so there was a tidy profit without much effort. In fact, I didn't even pay for the Amazon DVD's until I'd already received money from eBay.

Unfortunately, in the way Amazon's system works products are evaluated regularly and by the end of the year prices of this DVD increased to £11.97 each (see below). This meant that I had to move on to another product until the Amazon price dropped again. But it was nice whilst it lasted!

Because eBay allows you to put an item up for sale for 10 days and advises buyers to allow a further 10 days to receive the product I had a window of up to 20 days to sell and post a product even if it wasn't in stock! In fact, if a buyer purchased my product and paid immediately, I was able to receive the buyers money to purchase the product that didn't really exist in my shop. I'd then go ahead and purchase the product at cut price from Amazon with the buyers money and send the product when I received it. If I didn't sell enough to qualify for Amazons discount – I'd simply refund the buyers and cancel the transactions.

In actual fact, Amazon also allows you to send the product to a separate address so I didn't even need to handle a product myself if I didn't want to. Although this is only possible with single buys.

Anyway back to my experience. I took my DVD's that were purchased from Amazon with their cut price postage and offered them for sale on an auction style on eBay at .99p each. The products actually cost me £2.53p each including postage, so in order not to lose money I added £2.53p postage on each DVD. (£2.53p + .99p = £3.52p). If in the unlikely event that I only sold each DVD for .99p I'd make at least some money even when you take away my listing fee.

Later in this chapter you'll see more about how you can benefit from psychological techniques of adding money to postage rather than your listing that will help to bolster your profit margin.

In every case of DVD sales I was able to gain at least three or four pounds profit (but usually £15) whilst the DVD was simultaneously for sale on Amazon for a much cheaper price even when you take into account postage. If only the buyer took the trouble to open up another browser to check price comparisons on Amazon, they would have avoided paying over the odds!

This astounded me as the internet is an innovation that cries out to assist you in scouring the digital world for the best products at their best prices. Yet here was a site that drew you in and drew the buyers into an online battle to win an auction at any cost –often paying over the odds.

I began to get lazy, why should I wait ten days for the auction end? I began listing the product at a buy-it now price for an immediate profit, again no-one checked Amazon and I kept on selling. This is not unusual, this is business. If you pop down to your local £1 shop and buy a couple of products for a pound you will invariably find that a listing of 99 pence with a postage cost exceeding it's real terms will give you a reasonable profit. This is simply good business sense, just like in the real world of wholesalers and retailers.

It's often the case that bidders will pay well over the odds for your product and over its retail value predominantly because the buyer gets caught in a cycle of competition and excitement. You can use peoples emotions to try to get a good price in your sales with careful use of psychology.

People panic at the end of an auction and you'll notice that it is rare for an initial bidder who originally bid for your .99p product to actually win the item in the end. Usually they are not that serious and are just trying to get a cheap bargain with no intention of paying more. These people are great because once the ball is rolling other bidders will start to bid.

How to turn buyers into winners.

Creating a sense of urgency

Whenever you communicate with a bidder always create an air of excitement and develop emotional states of urgency. As with all sales make the customer feel important. It's more than making them want the product it's about making them feel they need it.

When somebody emails you a question again this person also rarely wins the final auction however, you can use their questions in your psychological war. Always post their question on eBay, there is a click box on the reply form which allows you to do this.

> It's more than making them want the product it's about making them feel they need it.

Posting questions makes other potential buyers think there are other watchers too and a sense of drama unfolds. Bidders cannot see the amount of watchers, only the seller can so it's important to make people feel the product is desirable. You can if you wish, create another user name and send yourself a question just to get this across.

> Although getting friends to bid on your product is illegal in eBay terms, getting a friend to ask questions on your auctions is fine and gives the illusion to real potential buyers that there are many buyers out there which increases the desirability of your auctions.

Also always use a counter and click on it as often as possible, try to get friends to click it up over at least 100 if it's on a 10 day auction.

You have to remember both with online and off line auctions, the consumer is not just another buyer as is the case in conventional shops, they are a 'winner' of their purchase. Being a winner is emotionally charged and if you can cultivate this state of mind before and even after your auction you'll get a better price and a returning customer. Not only has the winner won the product but they have 'beaten' other bidders. They have become the Champion!

> The consumer is not just another buyer as is the case in conventional shops they are a 'winner' of their purchase

Your description should be charged with a sense of urgency and uniqueness of product. Your product should be hinted at as being 'the last left' even if it's not.

A Change in Dynamics

A trait that the advent of online auctions have developed is the drift from the old dynamics of auction houses.

Gone are the days when auctions invariably consisted of rare, hugely expensive items most often antiques collected by specialist buyers. Today the type of product found on online auctions are often modern day items selling at low prices. EBay seems to encourage a low starting price and penalises the seller financially for setting a high price or even setting a reserve on a product. In fact during the latter part of 2006 you were no-longer allowed to set reserves on products under £50. This has now changed back- presumably too much revenue was being lost. Statistics show that a reserve price reduces the likelihood of a sale – more about this later. If you want to set a reserve it is more cost effective to set a high starting price.

EBayers need to get way from the perception that you must sell rare products to make large sums of money. If you research Power Sellers who have to retain a high amount of income to keep their status you'll invariably find low cost, large volume sales rather than one off antiques. The exception may be Auto sales although these often sell for below the market value that you may see advertised within local magazines and papers. It still makes me wonder why a reputable seller would list cars on eBay when one of the main attributes to buying a car is to check it over in person and more importantly listen to the engine and drive it. It seems to me that the only reason one would sell a car on eBay is that it would receive a higher price than if the buyer first checked it over. I'm not aware of any good reason a seller would prefer buyers to bid before looking at the product.

Having said this, the advent of 'classified car ads' on eBay is seeing a change in the way cars are listed and sold.

Market Place Evaluations

With the large inexpensive market place now available sellers need to be more vigilant of customer needs. Clearly in a market where so many identical or closely comparable products are easily available traders need to diversify even further than in a 'bricks and mortar' shopping market.

Considerations to be evaluated in an online market place are as follows;
- Distinguishing your product from others, quickly and cost

effectively.
- Making your product stand out and bid upon when multiple auctions end simultaneously.
- Making the buyer feel a sense of urgency to bid on your product even if you have a large stock of product available.
- Overlapping auctions.
- Considerations on buyers budget – they often refrain from bidding on multiple items that end close to each other just in case they accidentally win more products than they can afford. Buyers can withdraw a bid at the last moment, however, this does not make you very popular with other bidders or sellers and often results in disgruntled traders bidding up and dropping out of your auctions – retaliation.
- Listing in related, but lower volume categories to reduce competition.
- Future predicting - Bidders bid lower in auctions when a similar product is selling following the end of your auction. Or other auctions are assumed in the near future.
- Title Keyword Spamming – as discussed earlier adding keywords in a 'sentence' style you can dramatically increase sales and keep within the eBay rules.
- Time Zone considerations and day of week. – End days and times need to be considered as Thursdays and Sundays are generally the days to end an item on. But clearly other time zones are important if there is a large market in a specific country that you do not live. The American is a good example of a huge market where time zones can predict a bad end time if listing in England.

Profiting from Multiple Sales

In most cases of online auctions, bundling products is not as profitable as selling products separately. Bundling tends to reduce the amount of bidders as many people do not want multiple items or do not want to pay the higher financial outlay of buying more than one product. This said, there are times that bundling is worthwhile. Obviously if one is a wholesaler with extremely low costs it is sometimes feasible to resell bundles of products to other traders in order for them to sell the products on separately at a profit. However, this is rarely the case, most eBayers are there to purchase a product that they intend to use not resell.

In these cases *1 the only financially viable bundling technique is when the seller has to offer two or more products, one of which is more desirable than the other. Selling a more desirable product will increase the selling value of a less desirable product that the seller may have trouble shifting if not sold within a bundle.

Although it is difficult to predict the amount of likely bidders for a product, research suggests that in auctions with more than two bidders, separate component auctions are more profitable than a bundle sale. As most auctions consist of two or more bidders or at least watchers, it begs the question whether it is ever worthwhile selling a bundle of items. You can of course check the 'completed' auctions in the advanced search facility to see the performance of a previous product auction and try to predict the likely amount of bidders for your sale.

It may be noted that selling two differently valued items for profit will only work if the customers are aware of the higher products value. You can state this value in your auction especially if such an item has recently sold for more than its market value. In this case a link to the completed auction would be of benefit.

Research *2 also suggests that not making buyers aware of the worth of your lower value item within the bundle would be beneficial. People tend to assess the price as being higher when sold with a higher value product. But remember the buyer is usually concentrating on bidding for the higher value item and is not overly concerned with the other product.

In 2000 Milgrom and Weber *3 showed that with an auction consisting of more than one product sold in succession, each auctions sees a reduction in bidders because the winner leaves (assuming the winner only wants one item) and the bidders left bid higher than previously (but probably not higher than the first sale price), thus keeping proceeds static.

> It has to be said that online auctions are environments that lend themselves perfectly to addiction and just like gambling draw in a specific type of person who is eager to satisfy a myriad of emotional, psychological and physical needs.

Just like online gambling, auction sites through necessity often offer a perceived 'safe' environment where the computer user is invariably in familiar surrounds such as home or even the office. Familiar surroundings fool the user into a false sense of security when dealing with risk and may increase the likelihood of making larger more risky decisions that one might not dare to partake in, in the 'real' world.

Websites that offer potential risk and excitement often draw in people with social anxieties, people who are prone to depression, low esteem, social phobias and consequently loneliness. The anonymity and possibilities of hiding behind a persona offered by user ID's and feedback ratings create a colourful and dynamic world where some may not dare to venture in a face to face environment. Perhaps not all bad in that a virtual world is maybe more desirable than none at all, but it does beg the question would some of these hardened eBayers benefit from the 'cognitive behavioural' effect of having to face people and develop social skills in the event that there was not the virtual offerings in place?

Internet addiction is gaining its ground and although not formally recognized is set to be well on its way to its own category in the "Psychological Library".

There are many obvious psychological benefits to online auctions and the sense of empowerment must be a godsend to the low self-esteemers. People who would be denied the (often intimidating) participation of auctions in the real world.

Although initially anger may set in, eBay might be disappointed to discover many experience a great sense of relief when banned or suspended. From my own experience I was surprised to notice a sense of relief and the thoughts that 'at last it's all over' cross my mind when I found that I no-longer was able to log-on. It made me realise perhaps I had been spending too long maintaining my online shop when I could have been building my 'bricks and mortar' business or interacting with the real world in another way.

EBay's attempt at 'teaching me a lesson' for breaking their weak rules backfired with a realisation that I no-longer wanted or needed an income from their site and the closure of my shop became a permanent fixture. I still traded on eBay but without the fully stocked shop that feeds eBays endless quest to take a chunk of my income through monthly fees.

No more checking emails, no more watched items ready to be bid upon, no more ridiculous questions from apparently potential bidders etc. What a relief!

Virtual self–esteem

As one trades more and more on auction sites, particularly eBay, you will find that many normal traders who conduct themselves in a reasonable manner in the real world become aggressive and unreasonable in the virtual world.

The safety of trading in their own homes seem to create a 'virtual alter-ego' an elevated sense of self worth that is not necessarily conducive to good business. People act in a way they would never dream of in a face to face situation.

I had a very unreasonable and dishonest buyer who from the outset gave me the impression that he would be trouble. In these cases I always make sure I do everything 'by the book' and in particular get 'proof of sending' when I post an item.

My hunch was correct as he tried to claim all sorts of things that would either get him a refund or an extra product for free. His user ID was an indication of the sort mentality he had, I don't recall it exactly but I do remember it was along the lines of 'Cage fighter', 'Street fighter' or something like that. He obviously felt this might intimidate me when making threats. You'll notice many subtitle threats that are unspoken, but obviously made when communicating with these idiots.

His final trick to intimidate when he lost his eBay complaint case and had nowhere else to go was to ask eBay for my home address. When a trader requests your address eBay sends an email to the seller stating that they have sent it to the person making the complaint. You have no choice in this matter, but it is given away. (Personally I feel there could be Data Protection issues here however, I assume these are said to be covered in ones initial trading contract when signing up to eBay.) The buyer had no need for this information as he'd have received it when I sent the product however, it does insinuate that he may be going to 'pay me a visit'! It didn't work so we just left it at exchanging negative feedback and went on our way. I did ban this member from buying from me again though, which is an excellent facility that eBay rarely advertise, obviously it is not in their interest to stop people trading.

Go to http://cgi1.ebay.co.uk/ws/eBayISAPI.dll?bidderblocklogin or search eBays help pages for 'Block Bidder' to add someone to your own list.

Psychological of online auction participation

Sense of community

One psychological grip online auctions hold is the sense of control one perceives from partaking in group valuations. Both buyer and seller exert their power on the value of a product. Even if the auction, as it often does, flies out of control during the last moments. Buyers still have a sense that they bid on their own terms.

On eBay most sellers are encouraged to start bids at .99 pence. Consequently buyers enjoy a universally attainable price. A price that they are controlling by both their choice of bid price and the tactics they exert.

Having control of the value of an item is a luxury seldom afforded in the 'bricks and mortar' world that we had become accustomed. You enter a shop seeking the product that you desire and accept the price tag assuming this is a fair value. One seldom barters for a better price, this is not usually socially acceptable and breaking this 'code' is a way of breaking community rules. Of course, there are places where haggling is acceptable in the 'bricks and mortar' world such as market places, car boot sales and the like.

Online auctions have given the consumer a wonderful feeling of control and many "Darwinians" might subscribe to the ideal that this is a human trait essential to our health and mental stability.

This is one of the strong psychological glues that keeps the trader returning to the auction style formats both from a buying and selling point of view.

Addiction to excitement – seller and buyer addiction

We're all aware of the adrenalin rush instigated by gambling, risk taking and even computer games. Similar highs can be obtained by buying and selling online. The seller waits in anticipation as his item climbs incrementally in price – will he make a profit?!

EBay has been very clever to help raise the bar on this excitement for the seller by adding confidential information on how many potential buyers are 'watching' the item. This elevates the stakes in excitement when the seller has a fair idea that last minute bidders are hiding ready to pounce at the last moments of sale closure. In addition the seller has to make decisions on whether to pull out of an auction if no bid has been placed. Are there hidden bidders waiting to pounce at the last moment?

The greatest highs are on offer to buyers. Not only is a quest to bag yourself a bargain an addictive intention, but even when a buyer ends up in a bidding war and paying over the odds, winning traders can still revel in a sense of success. Satisfied at being the acclaimed winner in front of an audience of potential buyers.

Competing against rivals

There is little more compelling than the rivalry between auction bidders. With the nature of eBay you can easily spend more money than you can afford, satisfied with the knowledge that just by with holding payment for a few days you can build up the required funds by selling a few more items yourself to cover the shortfall. This is a massive incentive to win an auction at any cost and heavily paying more than intended. Unlike real life auctions where you need to either have the cash on you, or an account with the auctioneer, eBay does not require you to pay immediately (unless specifically requested). The human instinct of instant gratification is satisfied and proves to be very addictive.

Community Status and sense of belonging

There are many community values to an auction site such as eBay. A sense of community, status elevation through labels such as power selling, ID naming not to mention the feedback status one receives. Friends are also often forged through the sharing and bringing together of common interests of like-minded people.

Whether true or not, many eBayers perceive themselves as successful in their area of specialty. By comparing their level of feedback they can reveal in a sense of achievement that their online peers are rated at a lesser level. Although ones true value is unclear as some traders have multiple ID's.

A healthy sense of competition can develop as one traders aims to 'beat' another in sales targets, often becoming a temporary obsession.

Friendship

Although we've covered the emotional rush of being a part of group product valuations, friendships are also forged through mutual success or a sense of belonging from 'label status' that can often be equated to 'job titles' in the real world.

EBay's system of offering high volume sellers community status such as 'Power Sellers' or even high feedback labels, raises sellers online and off-line self worth. They feel they have the respect of other traders and eBay offers them extra support in their trading activities.

As we've already discussed once you are a Power Seller eBay treats you better than other traders on eBay. You can enjoy benefits such as an Account Manager who sorts out any problems, helps you gain the best exposure and obviously eBay Account Managers have access to statistics and marketing information that non-employees simple don't have.

There are of course, the unofficial benefits from having a 'good reputation' that feedback scores claim to offer. In the instance where there is a dispute between a relatively new seller with a poor feedback rating and a Power Seller who do you think eBay will avoid upsetting? Perhaps the one who makes them thousands of pounds per year and has a dedicated customer service assistant?!! - perhaps?

Perceptual Value

Bidders often change their perception of product value due to other bidder's perceived value, internal factors like personal motivation for auction participation, emotions during bidding.

Bidders also change their minds as to which products to bid upon based on seller reputation, although this aspect accounts for far less than most eBayers believe it to.

As we have seen traders are influence by other traders behaviour (just like in real life). The average seller suffers negative feedback after 129 transactions *4 (I received my first negative after 100, in fact it was exactly 101. Surprisingly there is little drop in sales due to a negative feedback comment and the drop in sales is due to the seller not the opinion of eBay buyers. Buyers seem to either not care or do not check for feedback before buying. The slight drop in sales is thought to be due to a reduction in effort by the seller after the disappointment in a negative. In fact the subsequent negatives in a seller's career will be mainly due to this newfound discouragement not from a poor reputation among buyers.

I personally found you could fight off subsequent negative feedbacks following the first by not giving feedback until it was first given to you. More about these techniques later.

Sellers advantages

Other psychological advantages that online trading may offer is the lack of real face to face negotiation or even social skills that some may enjoy.

The invention of online trading was a computer nerd's delight. No-longer did they have to leave the secure environment of their PC and face those awkward liaisons with the real world. At last they could now trade on an equal basis! Of course, as eBay grows the percentage of computer nerds that trade has reduced. Today people from all walks of life use it as a trading platform.

The same is true for those who have no intention of honing their real-life sales skills. EBay offers traders easy price negotiation technology. Send a simple email with your offer, or just place your maximum bid and walk away, eBay will place your bids in increments until you reach your maximum.

> The other benefit to some is the lack of need to conform to social etiquette. Although some would argue that eBay has an etiquette all of its own. Gone is the need to wear a suit to do business- in fact, you don't have to wear anything at all!

Selling and Ending items on Thursdays

The best day for internet traffic is on a Thursday this is the case across the board of websites. Obviously there are the weekends which also yield a good sales record but Thursday is the mid week champion. Generally on eBay it is claimed that Sunday is the best day for ending an item. However, this does depend on your item. If you are selling office equipment perhaps during the working day, mid week is more likely to get you a sale as the type of person buying is most likely to be purchasing during office hours.

There are of course good reasons for this and they reside in the workplace. It is an unfortunate fact that a vast majority of British workers are bored stiff in their jobs. It is also true that a large majority of internet users only have access at work.

Monday is a low traffic day due to the fact that people are just back from the weekend and have loads of work and phone messages waiting for them.

Friday is usually also low in traffic because some employees are keen to finish outstanding work before the weekend so they can relax; others have already begun to relax!!

Another aspect that you might like to consider is the varying time zones across the world when ending an item that is advertised internationally. If you anticipate a large US following for perhaps say, a hard to find product in a specific state. Then it would be fool-hardy to end the item in the day in your own country but ignore the fact that it's 4 am in the target county.

If your item is highly desirable in a foreign country, then spend a few moments checking the 'completed items' search section to see when similar items most often end. You can copy these time scales to replicate sales.

Moulding Kids into crooks

The longer eBay allows traders to con their way to successful trading the more ingrained this attitude will become. We are allowing a nation of fraudsters and gamblers to develop.

I can't blame the younger eBayers for the misconduct that saturates the website however, it is the younger generation who often fall victim to these scams. These are the people (as was the case with myself) who quickly and unintentionally learn these scams through this victimisation. They either protect themselves by using and being aware of the techniques discussed in this book or they become scammers themselves.

The exposure to these cons and the inevitable desensitisation that they evoke can create scammers from normally morally stable eBayers.

The safe environments and the ability to switch off the technology (a communication) at will helps to create aggressive, unrepentant traders. It is easy to con people and then close down your account to cease all contact with the seller; this has to enhance the temptation to make a 'quick buck'.

Reserve prices

Oddly, reserve prices often actually stop items being sold. Many buyers want to bid on their "own terms". They don't want sellers to insist on a minimum price. This is again just a psychological barrier but, a barrier that effect's real world trading prices.

When traders see that there is a reserve price they often ask the seller for the amount that the reserve is set to. Although this is allowed under eBay rules, this defeats the object of a hidden reserve and no seller is likely to disclose the amount. Buyers become frustrated and no longer wish to trade. They simply go else where.

What does seem strange is that if a seller sets a relatively high starting price but not a reserve price, buyers are happy to bid. This seems to be because a high starting price allows the buyer to remain in control and 'all cards are on the deck' there is no hidden values which is the case in reserve prices.

Facts;

1. Bidders rarely have a good understanding of a products real value.
2. Sense of community creates an addiction to eBay the type that we

often see in gambling.
3. Panic buying enables the seller to get a better price than with 'buy-it' now prices.
4. The majority of 'buyers' who ask you questions about your item do not end up buying the item.
5. Creating a sense of value, rarity and rivalry commands higher selling prices.
6. Ending times and days yield better prices.
7. Reserve prices dramatically reduce the likelihood of a sale.

*1 Popkowski Leszczyc, Pracejus, and Shen (2004).
*2 (Chakraborty 1999, Palfrey 1983)
*3 - Economics, Psychology, and Social Dynamics of Consumer Bidding in Auctions, Amar Cheema, Assistant Professor of Marketing, Washington University in Saint Louis
*4 P28, The Dynamics of seller reputation: Theory and Evidence from EBay.

SIX

The GREAT BIG eBay Hustle - Tricks to make you Rich

Private Listing to sell counterfeit products

Something that I noticed when researching this book is that some copyright owners watch people who sell their products and if the product is easily duplicated (such as with a DVD) they will allow you to sell only one copy. Often, they add you to 'favourites' in their eBay account so they get an email every time you list a new item. Thereby monitoring your selling behaviour. Once you have listed the second item they will have it removed as they say you would normally only have one. This is not always the case. When I researched this issue I had auctioned my product but not actually sold it. It seemed to have sold in my listing, but I then told the seller it was not available and refunded his money. When I re-listed, the copyright owner had my product removed and asked me for proof of purchase as I had already "allegedly" sold one and private sellers should not own multiple items – apparently! I did not bother to reply and just left it at that. The truth is that many eBayers buy and sell second hand products and could easily have multiple items.

One way to get around this problem is to list items in private listings. This way the copyright owners have no indication of who sold or bought the item. You can then re-list these over and over. I have noticed traders who continue to duplicate fake products under the noses of copyright owners by using this facility.

When you create a private listing the buyers ID does not appear in the listing. Only the seller can view the buyers User ID. The great thing about buying from a private listing (if you are intending to resell a counterfeit product and hide it from copyright sellers) is that the listing continues to be hidden in your feedback.

> So as long as you have multiple IDs you can sell fakes.

EBay attempted to up-grade the feedback system in 2007. However, they failed to iron out this problem. The new system as mentioned earlier, has seen the addition of the listing title and price in feedback comments. By using a private listing format these additions are hidden, which in my mind defeats the point of integrating the new system. As stated before eBay have now made all user ID's hidden in all listings but I believe this will make shill bidding even more rife so we should see this private facility return in the very near future.

To make your listing private:

1. Start creating your listing as normal using the Sell Your Item form.
2. On the Sell: Create Your Listing page, click the "Show/Hide Options" icon at the top of the page. A popup is displayed.
3. Under Item Details on the left, click "Format". You'll see the Private Listing option on the right-hand side.
4. Tick the Private Listing box then click the "Save" button. This makes the option available on the Sell: Create Your Listing page.

5. Scroll down the Sell: Create Your Listing page to the Selling Format section and tick the "Private Listing" option.

Shill bidding in Private Auctions

Obviously it is very difficult to detect shill bidding (bidding on your own auctions) if a traders User ID is hidden such as in Private Auctions. The problem here is that the main reason for private auctions is to hide the ID's of bidders on high value items in order to prevent other sellers approaching them with a similar product during the auction.

High value items are exactly the sort of product that attracts shill bidding, as the seller rarely wants to lose his product at a low price. Private auctions can hide shill bidding from the general public awareness.

Other legitimate reasons for private auctions are the sales of 'adult' products or embarrassing products that a buyer would not like others to see him purchase. Perhaps you don't particularly want to pop in to your local store to buy Pile cream and meet your next door neighbour in the process. Online purchases are an excellent forum for such transactions (assuming you have a soft cushion at your computer desk!) as long as you can avoid having the product in your purchase history – private auctions lend themselves very well to this.

The fact is that you need to get a bid on your item early in the auction in order for it to sell well. It is estimated that you will receive 1000% more clicks *1 once a bid has been placed. So starting the ball rolling is a good idea especially if there is a lot of competition in your chosen market place.

As of April 2008 all auctions have hidden ID's so private auctions will not be necessary. This may change again, as I feel this may cause a dramatic increase in Shill bidding – we will see.

Create a seller ring to sell fake products

Copyright owners can have your listing removed if you sell multiple items. Even they know that it is unreasonable to remove a product if a seller is genuinely trying to sell his own private products.

If traders have a desirable product, a DVD for instance, and are prepared to duplicate the product themselves, some hustlers have been known to ask friends to sell copies for a share in the profits. Often the hustler doesn't want them to sell in the same category, as this would mean competition and a reduction in their own final price. They wait until they have shifted as much as they can then hand over the selling to 'third parties' and receive a fee for supplying the product.

EBay and other authorities do look out for such trading rings but they are difficult to detect.

Lost in Post scam

This is where the buyer claims they didn't received the product sent and they attempt to get their money back, then sell the product on. This is very profitable as the buyer not only gets your product but their money is returned and they get to resell your product as well. In theory you should get insurance and more importantly some form of tracking on your merchandise so that you can prove you sent it. In reality it is often far too expensive to send all your sold items by recorded delivery as it would eat into your profits.

You can partially protect yourself by getting proof of sending, it's free. If a buyer pretends that they have not received the product all you need to do is to scan in the 'proof of purchase' obtained from the post office during posting and email it to the buyer. Often this is enough for dodgy buyers to concede and admit they have received the said item. I can't count the amount of times that buyers have claimed to not have received one of my CD's and backed down after a receipt is sent. Most often they will apologise and claim it has just arrived or somebody in their building placed it somewhere safe without telling the recipient!

The only problem with proof of purchase is that PayPal do not consider it as proof enough to win a dispute. They must receive a tracking number for the seller to win a 'lost in post' claim or the buyer will simply get their money back. This is a scam that many 'newbies' fall victim to.

Getting extra cash from watchers – if they don't bid

Many people will see a product at a price they like and just watch the product until it comes to auction. What they fail to do is check the item has not changed. A popular technique is to wait for your product to gain several watchers and then modify the listing to your advantage. Traders add a few pounds to the postage or add comments to the description that there is only one product for sale when previously you were selling two. Because eBay will allow you to modify your listing until it has been bid upon if people are being tight with their money by waiting until auction end – you can financially punish them!

The trick here is that people simply do not re-read the description as they were satisfied with it before (assuming they read it the first time), they simply watch it and bid at the last minute. And because in a dispute eBay will look at the final description not the one previously listed they will be on the buyers side in that all was described as indicated at the final sale.

This is why if I see an item that is good value I always make sure I bid upon the product when it's cheap (usually 99 pence) – I then know the seller can not alter anything to increase the hidden costs.

Feedback Blackmail

There are many ways Feedback can be used to 'backmail' traders and it's often the case that traders don't even need to make a blatant threat as seasoned traders are fully aware of the issue.

Most Powersellers will not give you feedback until you have given them positive feedback. This effectively stops bad feedback because traders do not want negative retaliation feedback. EBay do not allow you to have malicious feedback removed (except for extreme cases of offensiveness) even if it's clearly in retaliation to another traders negative feedback.

> If you never give feedback until you receive feedback then it is insinuated that you will retaliate and this is enough to insure a good reputation on eBay.

An issue you do need to take into account is that Powersellers are able to receive multiple feedbacks from separate products from the same buyer.

Until May 2008 this was not the case with 'normal' eBayers because with normal people if a buyer purchases three products from the same seller they are only able to give one level of feedback (that counts on the sellers ID). Powersellers can receive multiple feedbacks on IDs from the same buyer – hence Powersellers high feedback numbers. The changes in May mean that if a normal seller receives more than one feedback from a trader it accounts for extra feedback however, traders are restricted to one Feedback per week from the same trading partner. This is not the case with Powersellers who can receive as much as they like.

To powersellers each purchase is worth one feedback, to the hustler it is worth buying multiple items from a Powerseller as it will have more of an impact on his feedback rating – in fact it is possible to reduce his rating below that threshold to have his status taken away.

This is also a good technique if the hustler notices a Powerseller is right on his threshold, he is ideal to buy from as they know that they will get a good service and can threaten discreetly bad feedback for additional deals (see the next section).

How traders target Power sellers for blackmail

Although considered the holy grail of eBay Power sellers are excellent candidates for blackmail! But be careful because if eBay are going to take sides – guess whose side they are likely to support!

Powersellers must retain a certain level of financial turnover (£750 per month for the lowest bronze Powerseller) or to sell a specific number of products (100) to keep their Powerseller status. Now it's worth noting that these weirdo's are very proud of their label and often rely on eBay as their sole source of income. This marks them as ideal victims for getting the hustler a good deal although its worth remembering that most powersellers have a dedicated account manager on their side so traders need to be careful – one complaint to his account manager and you could be suspended. Account Managers do not work with Bronze Powersellers (the lowest level) who earn £750 per month, but all other Powersellers from Silver (selling £1,500 per month) to Titanium (selling £95,000 per month) have account managers assisting them. So it is best for hustlers to target Bronze Powersellers if possible.

If you have any problem with a product that a Powerseller sells you or even if you make up a problem they will bend over backwards to help you in order not to receive bad feedback. Good feedback is another aspect that Powersellers need to retain, at a level of 98% rating or above. If one Powerseller is on the verge of not making his targets that month he may give buyers discount or a refund even though they are in the wrong. He can't afford to lose his status.

Even if traders want to play fair. Powersellers are excellent people to track down as they often sell items at cut down price, sometimes even making a loss just so they can sell their monthly quota to remain a Powerseller.

The key here is always to be pleasant; if buyers go charging in shouting "give me this or it's bad feedback for you" it will get them nowhere and may backfire if he chooses to go to eBay. Insinuation is the key. When it comes to eBay, Powersellers have seen it all, buyers will lose if they get aggressive. They know the score, they understand their targets must be met.

Using PayPal to stop a traders income

This is another form of blackmail. Even if buyers have no claim or they are in the wrong making a PayPal claim can be very effective in getting a free income, even if they know that they are not going to win the claim. This is very effective towards Christmas.

PayPal allows buyers to make a claim without any real issue if they wish. The buyer can just file a claim under the guise 'significantly not as described'. Once filed the victim (the seller) has his PayPal account frozen which includes being unable to buy, sell or download their money into their bank account to use in the real world.

> Essentially this is one way PayPal uses your account to settle disputes. They are well aware that if a traders income is cut, even if they are in the right they will refund a buyer to their own cost just to get their income back. This clears up a lot of disputes for PayPal, so they benefit in not having to 'waste' staff time refereeing disputes.

Feedback 'loading'

This is a technique that allows you to feed hundreds of good feedback comments into your account so that poor feedback is relegated to the back pages. The issue here is that if someone is interested in your listed item and actually takes notice of feedback then they are unlikely to scroll past the second page. If they don't find bad feedback by then they are highly unlikely to read any further. This facility has been temporarily stopped however, there are still ways of loading good feedback as the principle remains the same and I suspect the facility may well make a return in the near future.

The trick here then is to get any recent poor feedback relegated to pages three or four which is about 100 feedback comments. You can easily do this by having multiple ID's set up. One of these ID's should be for getting positive feedback. You might just buy on this account so as long as you pay rapidly you should quickly build up a 100% rating- most bad feedback is left by buyers not sellers (unless retaliation). Once this is done wait until some idiot gives you bad feedback on your main account and simply transfer your 200 + feedback from your separate ID into your main account. You have then both successfully diluted your percentage rate on the main account and relegated the bad comments way back into page three or four where few people will bother to scroll through – job done, bad feedback will not affect your sales.

Previously eBay has again unsuccessfully tried to eliminate this practice by setting a 60 day stagnation period. Where by the account you would like to merge has to have been inactive for 60 days. But this is not a problem because everyone is allowed three accounts therefore hustlers can still carry on your shill biding etc with two accounts and leave the third inactive for several months ready for the merge when you need it.

As mentioned in 2008 eBay discretely banned account merging without an official announcement. I suspect that this practice will soon be reinstated once eBay realise that eBayers are unhappy with the loss of this tool, especially considering eBay banned this on the quiet!

The point is all you need to do when you receive bad feedback is too list several hundred inexpensive items that sell quickly. Make sure you give a good service and you will rapidly receive many positive feedbacks.

Poaching bidders

An excellent technique to find customers who might be interested in your products. Best used weeks after the auction that you are poaching from, but this depends on the type of product you sell.

If you immediately try to poach bidders it is easy for traders to inform eBay and eBay can easily see who you've emailed for poaching purposes. If you frequently have similar products for sale then it's easy to jot down the user names of those who have bid upon the item and leave it for a few days. You can then email these users in view to offer them a similar product. This will increase the amount of people bidding on your item or even make a sale off eBay saving you on eBay fees!! Win/win situation.

Again eBay 'completed listing' facility is a great way to source potential buyers and you know how much they are prepared to pay from their final bids!

Building an email database

Although this is not illegal on eBay they certainly do not like you building your own "off eBay" business. Obviously they are in the business to keep you trading through their website, this is one reason why traders email addresses are hidden.

It's a fact that past customers are more likely to buy from you again if they have had a good experience. Testament to this on my own website www.SportsHypnosis.co.uk. I have around 25% returning customers who buy again so I know they are good candidates to market to at a later date. This is even more likely if you specialise in a specific type of product. It is therefore very profitable to occasionally email an offer to your past customers to gain an additional sale. Even if you do this just once a year, for instance at Christmas, it is likely to yield you a hefty increase in sales, especially if you market a discounted special offer.

Clearly it's of benefit to have your own private website in addition to your eBay trading account, but not essential for this to be effective.

Keeping a database of eBay customers is essential for future sales, if you don't do this you are losing money. Another good source of email address farming is to ask sellers questions who are selling similar products to your self. They will often return your email with their private address which you should capture and use in the future for marketing campaigns. Keep a database categorised into areas that suit your business.

Another possible source of income is to sell your eBay email address database once it is large enough, to another person or company. This will not win you any friends (or customers), but you can make a good income by doing this. The value of your database increases if it is categorised. It could be categorised into type of buyer i.e. buyers of books, sports equipment or even by region/ country. A simple Excel spread sheet would be fine for this. It must be noted that data protection is a hot subject these days so if your intention is to sell on a database it is advisable to pop some small print into your auctions stating that addresses may be shared. Take a leaf from the banking industry – make the text so small and inconvenient to read that customers will not bother!

It has to be said this is not something that you want to do if (like me) you have a profitable business with a sense of fair play.

Switching products scam

This is done extensively on eBay and can often be categorised as the perfect crime- in that many people don't even realise it has happened to them!

The title suggests exactly what goes on here. This is another scam that often occurs with high end products such as computer components or electrical equipment.

This scam is initiated when a scoundrel finds that they have at home a product that is broken in someway. Obviously the scoundrel doesn't do as you and I would and pay for it to be fixed, but logs on to eBay to find another product of an exact match.

> The criminal simply goes onto eBay and purchases a product that matches his/her own product in style, colour and model.

All very good I hear you say, nothing wrong with that. The scoundrel then purchases the new product and pays promptly through PayPal and awaits delivery. This is where it gets nasty.

Upon receipt of said item the crook then claims the new product was damaged in transit or more usually that the seller has sent a faulty item. He then requests his money back from the seller or through PayPal and may initiate a claim. The crook then sends his original broken product back to the seller claiming a refund.

Not only does the scoundrel gets his money back but has swapped his old broken product for a new working model! Bargain!

Now the experienced eBayer will be aware of this scam and many eBayers now mark their products in someway, often with an infrared pen with a code only understood by themselves.

The problem arises here with newbie's to eBay who are often blissfully unaware of the scam and just accept their item back and refund the buyer. They are then left with burnt fingers, a useless item and severely out of pocket. Especially as they can no longer sell their broken item without getting it repaired!

Sniping

Named after army snipers who lay in waiting for the enemy. These people wait until the last moments of an auctions end and slyly bid at the last minute. Although strictly not allowed by eBay this is the predominant method used by experienced eBayers to bid on products.

This technique does lead to lower auction prices which is exactly why everyone does it. Why would you bid on an item from the outset of the auction if it meant that you'd pay a higher price? You wouldn't!

For hardened eBayers who want a good deal there are various sniping software programmes that claim to bid within fractions of a second of an auction end. So even if another trader has ideas of out sniping you your software should prevail.

Sniping is impossible to regulate as it's difficult to distinguish whether somebody laid in waiting for the auction end or they have approached the auction at the end by accident. Especially as eBay encourage buyers to purchase at the end of auctions by advertising 'ending soon' auctions. EBay actively enhance this practice by holding 'nearly ending' auction advertisements on the front page encouraging people to visit auctions that are about to close.

Not all snipers win, it's the highest bidder who wins so if you wait until the end of an auction you may be too late. If you really want a product, leave a high bid from the outset and let others bid up in increments.

Again this is a strategy that eBay could do more to stop if they wished, but I would assume they would lose a large amount of their customers as it's this effect that creates the buzz eBay holds over buyers and sellers.

A part of the problem here is the Proxy bidding and the other part is the 'hard close rule' that eBay offers. The hard close is the fact that auctions end at a specific second which is predetermined. On some other auction sites there is a 'soft close' which research *2 suggests reduces the complaint. It also found that, with experience, eBayers tend to snipe more often.

Some studies [3] found that 20% of final bids were submitted in the final hour. In fact in some categories 59% of final bids were placed during the last 5 minutes.

[1] (Lucking –Reiley, JEP 2000)
[2] Roth and Ockenfels (AER, 2002)
[3] Sean Grey New York University and David Reiley University of Arizona.

Selling non-refundable products and services

EBay have a policy of not refunding for services or digital downloaded products no matter what the complaint.

Following is PayPal's response to a claim I made against a trader who did not deliver an electronic service that I had paid for. Needless to say I did not get my money back!

Case ID: PP-179-380-338
Transaction Amount: -206.80 GBP
Seller's Email: *with held,*   Seller's Name: *with held*

PayPal; Unfortunately, we were unable to resolve this claim in your favour because the item purchased was virtual or intangible. As a result, we have not taken any action against the seller at this time but we have noted your dissatisfaction in the seller's record for future reference.

Thank you for your cooperation with our investigation.

Thank you.

Protection Services Department

For example; The hustler could decide to sell a database of email addresses for marketing purposes and not to actually send the product. When the Buyer complains the seller keeps the money anyway. PayPal will always side on the seller in this case. They simply do not refund for these type of products. So listing these can yield the eBay conman a good income.

Obviously it won't make the trader any friends, but as long as the product they sell is desirable they could make a lot of money. Sooner or later eBay will remove their product if they keep getting complaints but they could always use a separate account.

From a quick search on eBay you will see that many people sell digital downloads from music mp3's to PDF files. Buyers are often blissfully unaware that they have no come back if the seller decides not to send or give access to downloads if they are digital in nature.

In fact there are thousands of people selling electronic items on eBay through click-bank. Most are honest traders some making huge incomes. Indeed digital downloads are an excellent form of income for the eBayer if they don't want to go through the hassle of posting products on a daily bases.

Selling CD's and DVD's

Obviously the copying of CD's and DVD's is rife. EBay are actually coming to their senses and did not allow standard refund policies for these products on their (now closed down) site eBay Express.

My main business on eBay was selling Hypnosis CD's for which I own the copyright, so it is clear that I am keen to protect my rights to stop them being illegally copied and distributed freely – this is quite easy in that they have both my voice and subliminal material on them. Even so, I always added a disclaimer to my auctions stating that there was a non returnable policy unless damage had occurred. Even then no money would be refunded but a like for like replacement offered but only if I received the damaged product back. It is amazing how many people claim the product is damaged and then when I state this policy, decide not to send it back for a replacement – I think this speaks volumes about the authenticity of the claim!

Such a policy added to your listing protects you to some degree however, upon a complaint to PayPal they are still likely to go against you and refund the money themselves from your account.

To reduce this possibility you should offer a replacement deal communicated through eBay emails. This is so PayPal can see your 'good will'.

Ten Day Listings

You may have noticed many eBay sites (each country has its own) charge a premium for listing an item for sale on a 10 day listing over a 3, 5 or 7 day listing. Although many eBayers are unaware, eBay know that a Ten day listing will yield you on average a *4% higher sale price*.

So if you can afford it always list for Ten days but make sure your item is on the first or second page of eBay during Thursday or the Weekend – this depends on how many other products are listed in your category.

As stated earlier, Sunday is generally the best day to end an item. But time zones need to be considered also. Many foreigners will bid on your item if it ends too early in the morning for them to bother staying up. This way you get an early bid (to get the bidding started) which also often has a second maximum bid which will encourage nationals to bid up higher than they usually would. It is always worth selling worldwide even if you are not willing to post abroad. You need the traffic and bids to get your auction going. So if you don't want to ship abroad set a ridiculously high international shipping cost, that way you may get an initial bid whilst the item is cheap but they will back out as prices rise.

The Buyer is King

Stopping a trader from winning a dispute (and getting their money back)

There is nothing more frustrating than some scally making a false complaint against you and running to eBay or PayPal for a refund. If the complaint is of the nature that a refund is inevitable traders often like to do the following.

Withdraw their money so buyers can't get it back – you've got 10 days for a dispute but your assets are frozen until the dispute is resolved. PayPal takes 5-7 days to withdraw funds from your bank account so you are going to need to hold off the traders complaint for a week. As long as you are nice to the person and insinuate a refund you should be able to put them off starting their complaint. If they are obviously 'taking the mickey' you might like to promise to refund them once you have enough cash in PayPal. If they accept this get your PayPal cash downloaded so they can't get their grubby hands onto it. Be careful not to offer them money back via eBay email as the refund will be given if you have accepted their terms. Communicate with them off eBay and deny ever agreeing to a refund.

How to win a product at the last minute

How to win a product at the last minute – decide the maximum price you are willing to pay, put your highest bid in about 5 seconds before the end of the auction - eBay only goes up in small increments so unless someone else bids up to your price you are likely to win, and if you don't, it doesn't matter as you didn't want to pay more than this anyway. You need to put your maximum bid in around 10 seconds before auction end to prevent other buyers bidding up to gauge a feel on your maximum price. They won't bid up too high they will just test small increments to see how high you have bid, eBayers are notoriously tight with their money so if you really want a product just put a high bid in that you can afford and in almost every case the auction will not go up to that amount. This technique seems simple but because the large majority of eBayers are skinflints you can always win products that you are serious about buying – just offer a fair price.

Make sure you leave such a small amount of time before auction end that tight eBayers bidding up in small increments don't have time to put enough small bids in to get to your maximum.

What to do if you get banned

Anyone worth their weight on eBay has a ban or suspension under their belt! Sooner or later some bitter eBayer that has lost a dispute with you will keep an eye on your account and make a complaint for a small misdemeanour. The first suspension should be for only 7 days and is not going to break the bank. You can then appeal if you wish. It's not in eBays interest to ban people for long as it's not just you losing money!

When your account is suspended eBay invariably suspend all your ID's so trading is impossible. You can't even buy a product on eBay.

Most traders find it quite easy to carry on trading. Assuming eBay has done their job correctly and banned all of your accounts, which is not always the case. If one of your ID's is still active just keep on trading on that account – your PayPal account should remain active.

Use someone else's account

If you are indeed fully banned get a friend or member of your family to open an account for you to trade from. Personally when I was banned I simply opened an eBay and PayPal account in my mothers name and continued to trade as before. You don't need to use their credit card details as PayPal allows you to open one without a card. Simply build up your money in your 'mother's' new PayPal account and transfer the cash to your old PayPal account to download into your bank.

Alternatively if all of your family and friends already trade on eBay it might be worth selling your products on their account and offering them a cut from the profits. The added advantage to them is that they gain some addition positive feedback - assuming you behave yourself!

Get a trading assistant

The truth is eBay can be a lot of hassle and it can be much easier to get someone else to do the listing, answer emails and deal with complaints in return for a small percentage of your products fee.

Get a trading assistant to trade for you, you find them on eBay in the Trading Assistants Directory.

They will often agree to work in whatever manner you wish and take pre-agreed fees. Personally I prefer to post my items so that I know how much has been sent and I can then check to make sure it correlates to how much the Trading Assistant has sold on eBay. This is due to the type of product I sell – CD's – as they can easily be duplicated and the Assistant could be selling far more than I am being told. However, this is not the case with most products. It is usually best to let the Assistant post so that there is no argument about whether you have posted the item that they have received payment for.

When using a Trading Assistant it is often best to give them the product and let them get on with it, that way you just collect the money!

http://tradingassistant.ebay.co.uk/ws/eBayISAPI.dll?TradingAssistant&page=main

SEVEN

The GREAT BIG eBay Con - Case Studies and how they do it

How the author made £450 in one weekend (equivalent to £164,000 per year) with fake software!

If you are looking for computer software on eBay that has a recommended retail price of hundreds or even thousands of pounds, and you find it on eBay for a tenner – rest assured it's fake! Now, many people are happy with this as they are getting the use of a product for a small fee. Probably a product that they would not usually be able to afford or use. And arguably companies benefit, just like those who offer student discount on software. The buyer pays the full price later on in life when the software is a requirement of working life or becomes commonplace in the working environment and practitioners have to use such software for business.

> In fact, statistics say that 35% of the worlds software is fake, so there is a huge percentage of the worlds population who feel it is acceptable to use fake products or just have to have the skills but can't afford the extortionate retail prices. I would imagine this percentage to go up if more people new how to get fake software.

Whilst researching this book I decided to give this a try, as eBay claim to be able to regulate their own site for fraud. I felt it was essential that I discovered what it was like and the barriers set in place as a con man on eBay. I found some PC software that retails at around £1,500 new. I duplicated the product and listed it for £15.00. I was inundated with messages, mostly asking if I had a crack or code so that the software would work – in other words the buyers were aware that it was fake.

The first CD sold instantly. I relisted another, then another, and literally as fast as I listed them they sold. I stopped selling at 30 CD sales which netted me around £450 in one day. That would make me an income of around £2500 per week. Obviously the market would probably dry up as there are only a limited number of potential buyers. Also this was during a weekend I'd probably not sell £450 everyday of the week. Nevertheless it's not a bad income from selling someone else's product that you are duplicating yourself!

It amazed me that it was so easy to sell dodgy products and make easy money on eBay. In fact, I could have gained a part-time income that most would not be able to achieve even working a full time job. It appears that even if someone had complained to me about the product I merely had to refund that single person and carry on as before. Most people who buy fake products such as this will look at your trading history and note that you have sold a hundred or so in the last week and realise the product was a counterfeit. As I've mention before in this book, eBay do not even remove a counterfeit product from your listings if a buyer complains. The VeRo programme only allows copyright owners to make a complaint about their own product and to have them removed. And by the way the Vero programme takes several days so if you list a fake item and the copyright owner is not a member of Vero you can get several days selling under your belt before a complaint is upheld. What happens in this instance is that the purchasers are emailed by eBay that they bought a counterfeit. And that's it. Money is not refunded so you keep your cash, and copyright owners won't sue you as it too expensive for one little eBay trader. Plus they are satisfied with the fact that your listing has been removed. They 'won' the battle.

> Incidentally, all buyers of my fake CD's were re-reimbursed and an explanation that this was a research process for my book given (and no animals, women or Children were hurt during the research process!)

The hardware they needed – CD printer, CD duplicator, CD Jewel cases, case printing paper, guillotine, scanner, PC. Printable CD's/DVD's.

The GREAT BIG eBay DVD rental service! - Cheaper than Blockbuster!

This is simple and eBay always give a refund. They are beginning to catch onto this trick and have made sure it doesn't happen on their new site eBay-Express. On eBay express you must have a refund policy on all products except CD's and DVD's. This is because of the ease at which you can copy these products.

To get the movie of your choice is simple and you don't need to partake in illegal activity by copying it.

Simply order it, when it arrives watch it and then send it back for a refund. It will cost you the price of postage back to the seller at the most. Much cheaper than Blockbusters! And you can use your saving to buy some popcorn!

The GREAT BIG eBay Business Loan!

If you need stock to furnish a new business venture then the Great BIG eBay Business Loan may be what you are looking for? It's not a new concept in the real world, buying and selling products before you actually have them in your possession and thousands already do this on eBay. What it does for you is allows you to 'stock-up' in your eBay shop, products that you do not have. Or more importantly, sell products that you do not have and can not afford to purchase. It's a way of kick starting your business or expanding an already established business.

The key here is not so much gaining the money but putting off buyers of your product so they do not make a complaint to eBay for a refund. Most people will wait a few days or even a week until they contact you about the problem. Even if they do contact you immediately by eBay's advice the buyer is asked to wait 10 days for delivery before a complaint can be made (the law on this varies from country to country and state-to-state). This gives you a window of 10 days, plus if a dispute is initiated PayPal allow a 20 day time frame to escalate this dispute to a claim. PayPal then take at least a week to make a decision over a claim and often it ends up more like several weeks because they usually email the buyer with a further question and give them an extra week to reply.

Usually you will have gained around a month of credit before there is a problem and if you are a smooth talker you won't get any complaints. You have to remember the buyer wants you to send the product, you have their money and because you didn't leave feedback when they purchased it, they will be eager not upset you too much.

You've now gained one month to spend £1000 as you wish. You have bought £1000 of products, resold them within that month, given everyone their money back, apologised for mix up and offered to trade good feedback. Your 'reputation' stays intact!

Of course you don't need to actually send any products at all, you can if you wish just refund everyone once you have bought and sold the products that your business needed.

Remember; just like the perfect crime, it's most effective if you only do this once with this account, so make it worthwhile!

You can as many eBayers do, use a separate User ID if you think that you are going to have problems delivering on time. This way you get the loan without harming the feedback on the main account that you are borrowing the money from.

The GREAT BIG interest free eBay personal loan!

This is similar to the business loan but you are buying something for yourself – after all you deserve it!

By using eBays policies of investigation you can gain access to other peoples money and eBay will kindly freeze the loan for you to spend at your leisure, whilst they 'look into it'. You would have to pay the money back in a couple of weeks but let's worry about that when it comes!

Case Study

Gerry had his eye on a new car (new to him anyway) for some time but in reality couldn't afford it. EBay were offering a solution. It was too difficult to buy one on eBay due to the likelihood of eBay freezing money during investigation. Not to mention the risk of buying a car on eBay without the option to give it a once over in person.

No, a purchase had to be made in the real world, a car dealership was quickly found with such a handsome specimen. Now all Gerry needed was some money!

On to eBay he logged. The key was to quickly make £20,000 and download it into his bank account before products were dispatched or complaints made. High end goods were the order of the day. Goods that did not exist of course!

Gerry was a nice kind of guy and wasn't about to rip people off, he just wanted to borrow the money for a few weeks and pay them back.

One of the best ways to source products that sell well for high prices is to check out how many sales others are getting. Copy their listing categories etc to duplicate their sales. You can research these in the completed listings in the 'advanced search' option of eBay.

It takes 5 days (minimum) to download the money from eBay so Gerry had to put people off making a complaint for at least five days or his assets would be frozen. This was even easier as it was August 2007 and postal strikes were rife. A great excuse to 'put off' potential buyer complaints.

This is how it works;

- 5 days download money.
- EBay request that people leave 10 days for delivery or response before making a complaint. – so he had an additional 5 days to play in the car or sell it.
- Complaints procedure; as we've said disputes allow 10 days (unless you can sweet talk yourself more time), assuming the dispute is escalated to a complaint, takes around 10 days.
- If Gerry doesn't have a bank account registered on PayPal,

PayPal cannot automatically take back money from the account. They only have access to money in his PayPal account of which funds were already withdrawn to purchase the car!

Triple your sales and profits from VHS Videos!

VHS Videos being the outdated technology that they are, sell for very low prices on eBay. Traders are keen to buy the new blockbuster release or educational video on DVD. So if the hustler has a video then there is a simple way to sell them at higher prices without getting into trouble with copyrighters.

The easy way to making a profit from Video sales: They simply sell 'back-up' copies of the video on DVD to increase video sales.

On eBay you can buy videos cheap and sell them for higher prices when a DVD is included. This does still seem to be an infringement of copyright laws but the law is difficult to clarify and seems a bit 'grey' if the product is sold as a 'backup' copy. Having said this, on eBay it is highly unlikely to have a complaint made of your auction if you sell the real item with a 'back-up' copy on DVD. Realistically if you have an original video and the product was once brought legitimately then having a 'back-up' on DVD is hardly the crime of the century, certainly not something Trading Standards would see as worth spending their limited budget on chasing.

You'll see that many eBayers use this technique but are discrete about advertising the DVD backup. This is because copyright owners can have your listing removed if they see it. It is one of the lesser known eBay rules, but if the seller puts the fact that he will send back up copies as well in the description most copyright owners will not bother reading all the text. In fact none of them will unless you are already known to them! If they check eBay they will simply see a title for a legitimate video and move on.

This is also a profitable way for the hustler to sell rare video formats to other countries thus opening up a much larger audience to your auctions sales. A British Video will not play or sell to a USA market, however, if you include a DVD the US buyer will happily bid for your product as DVDs are often universal in their ability to play.

The hardware they needed – CD printer (optional), CD Jewel cases, PC. Video recorder connected to your PC and TV software. The hustler is not trying to fob these DVD's off as the genuine article, so there is no need to print them and supply cases if they want to keep costs low. These are intended as back-up only so any cheap recordable DVD will do.

The product is secondary as this is merely a marketing exercise and to be honest the worse their DVD back up is, the less likely the buyer will resell on eBay and the less likely it will be that they have an additional competitor!

Free DVD's and your money back!

There are many specialist products on eBay that sell for high prices. One such product that I researched was a boxset of training hypnosis DVD's. These retail at £180 for 5 DVD's on eBay so secondhand copies are still fetching over £100 - £140 and sometimes even exceeding new prices true to eBay's panic buying format.

Case study

Jenny was a keen hypnotherapist and had read much of a particular authors work. However; the authors DVD's were out of her financial budget. She was keen to watch the DVD's and decided it was worth getting a hold of a copy.

Having seen a set that was clearly counterfeited she knew that all she needed was to find one hundred odd pounds for a week or so and then claim the funds back. She could afford to do this as long as she got the money back.

To check the DVD's were not real she sent an email to the seller asking the question outright "are these genuine?". It is clear that if a seller fails to respond to such a question it's highly likely that they are counterfeit.

The seller did not respond so the plan went ahead.

Jenny made a bid and eventually won the auction. In the meantime she had accumulated enough sales to cover the cost of these DVD's.

Jenny paid and the DVD's were dispatched to her address. Upon arrival and inspection the DVD's were clearly counterfeit, the labels were not of high quality and the DVD's had a purple backed dye. She knew that real DVD's of this kind had silver backs and were printed with ink onto the actual DVD face rather with paper labels – most legitimate manufacturers produce CDs and DVDs with silver dye on the reverse.

Armed with her evidence she knew she could get her money back. She was twice as excited because the DVD's all worked perfectly, so she could sit back and enjoy the product for free.

Jenny considered copying the DVD's but was concerned that the seller may get annoyed when she claimed the money back and she didn't want to incriminate herself with fake DVD's on the premises. Although Trading Standards were unlikely to investigate one set of DVDs she still felt uneasy having them around the house.

Once she had seen all the DVD's and intellectually absorbed all that she required, Jenny got back onto eBay and contacted the seller with her shock news that she felt the DVD's were fake. Jenny was hoping for a refund without the need to involve eBay or PayPal and was sure that the seller would not want to highlight their illegal selling of merchandise! She knew this did not have to be a one off scam, as long as she kept all her emails off the eBay system (which the fake DVD producer will be keen to do). No-one is likely to know how many times she has done this. She needed to request that the seller refunds her through PayPal as if paying for any other item or service.

She was correct in her assumptions. The seller duly offered a free refund in exchange for the DVD's back (to get rid of the evidence) and good feedback from Jenny.

This was acceptable and as planned so the refund transaction went ahead and products returned.

Jenny had successfully and 'legitimately' borrowed and watched the DVD's of her choice without paying a fortune. In addition she attained good feedback from the seller and she returned good feedback – after all it was a pleasant and fruitful transaction!

There is often no real reason to make complaints in these matters because the seller is keen not to have their account frozen for months on end whilst being investigated. Hustlers could if they wished ask the seller to give them a partial refund as it was not a real product – after all they did use the product.

The hardware they needed – none, other than low moral standards! Of course they could copy the DVD's for their own leisurely consumption if they are happy to have counterfeit products on their premises.

Making a quarter of a Million a year selling Tony Robbins CD's!

Whilst researching this book I have come across many sellers offering fake products but one stood out over the rest. The seller uses multiple ID's to sell counterfeit Anthony Robbins CD's. Not unusual in itself however, the reason I highlight this is that for those who do not consider this to be worthwhile or profitable think again. This trader was selling around 480 CD sets per week, although only making an estimated ten pounds per sale they were still turning over in the region of £20,000 worth of CD's per month. £250,000 per year - that's staggering! For someone to make that sort of money from another persons work is obscene, but eBay is the platform that allows this.

All the crook needs to do is find a valuable product that has copyright owners who do not monitor eBay – at this time Anthony Robbins seemed to be one of these.

I can understand why people do this in the short term. After all, from the evidence that I have seen from counterfeiters who have been caught on eBay all of them are offered a warning by Trading Standards before prosecution. If they stop trading following this warning they have few problems. It is only the ones who continue who end up with a criminal record.

The main reason many are getting away with it is that nobody complains. The four main components to this is that one: they are

Powersellers, so people assume the product is legitimate: two; they print fairly good quality CD's. CD's that most people cannot distinguish from the real thing. Three: buyers are aware that due to the low price in comparison to the real product the product is probably fake and the buyer is just happy to listen to the CD at a cut price. Four: eBay does not allow you to complain about fake products through the VeRo system- only copyright owners can do this.

One clue of a fake CD is that no packaging is included in these transactions. The CD's are sent in paper sleeves. This is most often a big clue to fraud. If the retailer is legitimate they usually will explain why the CD's are not packaged. Ex-display, damaged boxes etc. But this is rare, if boxes are damaged most sellers will sell the product listed as in a damaged box!

The equipment they needed – CD printer, PC.

In this case they would not be trying to pass these products off as real, but without packaging. So a good quality CD printer is required. The key here is to use a Thermal printer rather than inkjet. Thermal printers offer the same results as production companies who produce professional CD's. The CD's you buy are the same, but a little thinner than home CD's and silver on both sides. The printing has an etched look and can't smudge. These are best used for CD's that only have text rather than pictures. It's a low cost solution as the ink comes in only four colours and prints very thinly.

Ironically they can buy all the equipment they need to make fake CD's on eBay!

EIGHT

GREAT BIG Hustlers who didn't get away with it - and the mistakes they made

Nine case studies

EBay claims to have over 1000 staff in customer support and safety including an ex-Scotland Yard Detective liaising with the Police and monitoring unusual behaviour. However, it seems that it is easy to use other peoples' money to achieve your own gains. Especially if you keep a good relationship with the other trader and make sure you give the money back. The cases that follow show how easy it is to con people on eBay even if you are stupid and continue to steal money without ensuring a satisfactory solution between yourself and the trader to avoid a complaint to either eBay or the police.

The fact is, there is such a great deal of auction fraud going on in cyber space (with the large majority conducted on eBay) if you are sensible you will get away with it. If you don't receive complaints by others – i.e. you keep good customer services, if you borrow money and always give it back, and if you don't get greedy the authorities will leave you alone. They are looking for the big fish and the persistent offenders. Remember those who have been imprisoned were done so following consistent warnings that they chose to ignore. If they had ceased illegal activities when at the first, or even after second warnings they would have avoided imprisonment or even a fine.

Following are several case studies of how not to do it!

16 year old sold £50,000 worth of 'virtual computers'.
One case of a creative teenager who used a similar 'loans' scheme as I explained previously was a 16 year old from Wales.

This fraudster 'conned' hundreds of victims by selling non-existent electrical items on eBay. As the boy grew more and more confident in his quest for 'free' money he made the mistake of taunting his victims with a lavish lifestyle and abusive emails confirming his dodgy transactions.

One grave mistake was contacting victims via email stating his purchases and mocking them for their stupidity.

The teenager, admitted one hundred charges of fraud at a youth court in Wales, his activities were highlighted by complaints from eBay buyers who obviously never received the items they purchased. On the first occasion the boy settled the case against him out of court. However, following subsequent complaints he was put on Police bail.

When the teenager refused to stop his transactions and continued to sell non-existing goods he was arrested again.

The boy insisted that the site gave him a buzz and he was addicted to this sensation.

Even in the light of this case eBay insist that it is a safe place to trade with a former Scotland Yard Police Officer investigating unusual activity on eBay to weed out fraudsters.

From my research whilst using eBay and with cases like these coming to light it's impossible to believe eBay is doing all it can to battle fraud. My case is strengthened by the fact that you are supposedly unable to trade on eBay unless you are 18 years old. This boy was 16 years old and from my experience with sellers a huge amount of traders are under age. The immaturity of some traders is one difficulty (along with low IQ) I have encountered in negotiating with sellers when a transaction is unsatisfactory. Many under age traders just don't seem to have the life experience to see right from wrong and are being programmed and rewarded by lying and cheating. Trying to put across ones point of view is often futile.

Some would say that the size of eBay makes it virtually impossible to police 24 /7. And I would agree to some extent however, the vast amounts of profits enjoyed by eBay begs the question 'can't they afford more staff and monitoring systems?' You have to remember that each country runs its own eBay much like a small branch, probably not too hard to monitor. Especially with today's technology.

We can't expect the teenage generation not to try it on. They see some free pocket money to be made easily from their own bedrooms and seize the moment; the consequences are delayed and easily drawn out…

Like all convicted criminals this boy got too greedy and shot himself in the foot by mocking his victims.

What he did wrong… Clearly he wasn't going to win any friends by conning people and then taunting them, let alone sending incriminating emails confirming his dodgy transactions. EBay always uses emails as a tool for investigation and if you abuse people that is a sure way to get yourself banned and or prosecuted. It will always be an easier task for prosecutors to take you to court if you admit your crimes in writing, this person is a fool. Add to this the fact that courts always lean more softly towards the criminals who shows remorse. Taunting your victims will seal your fate when being sentenced.

Off line this fraudster displayed a lavish lifestyle that will always get you unwanted attention from neighbors, at least look like you are getting cash from a legitimate source!

Source; Steven Morris, Tuesday October 12, 2004 - www.guardian.co.uk" - The Guardian

Selling £100,000 of fake goods.

In 2005 a man was jailed for nine months for making his own counterfeit branded products and selling them on eBay.

Simon Hurley branded his own cigarette lighters, sun glasses cases and other engravable merchandise from his key cutting business in London. He is reputed to have sold over £100,000 worth of fake designer brands such as Gucci, Harley Davidson and Ray-ban and continued to do so even after several warnings from Trading Standards.

Following a Police raid on his business instigated by Trading Standards and the seizure of fake goods and equipment the man continued to trade counterfeit products on eBay. A subsequent raid was conducted and he was charged under the Trade Marks Act 1994. He will serve another two years imprisonment if he does not pay a large percentage of the money back to his customers. A bit of a shame really as the majority of his customers would have been happy with and well aware of the authenticity of his products.

It seems perhaps eBay's innovative anti-fraud technology wasn't working in this case. It seems to me that this case should never have gone to court. When Trading Standards seize goods from a trader eBay should be responsible and stopping all further trading. They failed to do this and allowed the perpetrator to continue his activities. Another testimony to the view that eBay are more interested in making money than regulating their market place.

Indeed eBay claim they are merely a 'venue' for buyer and sellers to trade and not responsible for their actions. I wonder if a 'Bricks and Mortar' shop would have the same attitude?

What he did wrong... As with most criminals who get caught this candidate got greedy, he already had a thriving business not to mention the high profit margin he was enjoying from his eBay scam. After making hundreds of thousands from his scam and being warned to stop – he would have been fine if he'd just stop the illegal stuff and spent his ill gotten gains. But no, he got greedy and foolishly carried on- jail and the confiscation of much of his wealth was the result.

* Fraudster jailed over eBay.con, http://www.zdnet.co.uk, Oct 7 2005 - By Lucy Thorne

Theft charges following eBay scam.
The following case is testimony to my research stating that; for eBay hustlers to make large amounts of money quickly through an eBay scam, the easiest way is to sell high end products that shift quickly. This is not always the case, CD's and DVD's are an excellent source of income if you can find highly desirable products.

A 27 year old American was charged with defrauding buyers from around the world in one of the largest internet frauds currently known.

Criminal complaints listed nearly $500,000 worth of non-existent products being sold through eBay. The Seller had been operating a legitimate computer sales business for over two years but then stopped sending out sold products. He continued to sell products without shipping them for three months leaving a trail of eBay complaints to the tune of 170 international buyers.

County prosecutors said he had outstanding computers, laptops and computer parts ranging from around $1,900 to $6,000 each.

He faces up to 24 years in prison.

Source: (Reuters), www.cnn.com

What he did wrong... This person seems to have become so overwhelmed by the amount of business that came his way through eBay that he just stopped supplying the winners. The nature of eBay can overwhelm those who suddenly see themselves with large amounts of customers bidding on their items.

When supply runs out but the seller has already received the money it's often hard to give that cash back. The bigger the backlog that accumulates the less likely one is going to fulfill the original orders.

Depending on the value of the purchase some sellers will give up trying to get their money back, but most will want a refund after several weeks. A partial refund sometimes satisfies and you get to keep the fees or even postage costs. Disgruntled buyers will often accept defeat if they get the majority back.

Police raid home of alleged eBay thief.

Although I've said that it is rare that small misdemeanors are followed up by fraud investigators you may be surprised by the next case study.

An American man had his house raided by Police following a tip off by the Internet Fraud Complaints Center.

It is alleged that he sold non-existent books and sports cards. The first complaint filed was for a book of the paltry sum of $32.00. The cheque was cashed but the book never arrived.

Police were later informed by eBay that the thief's account was terminated. As in other cases of fraud this seller was previously a good trader on eBay with 276 feedback comments of which only 16 were negative. This was the 16 currently being investigated!

This would normally indicate a lack of reliability in the feedback mechanism however; further investigation shows that in all of the cases of fraud, trading was conducted via cheque payments rather than credit card/ PayPal. The thief saw cheque payments as an easy way to defraud, clearly failing to consider the ease at which cheques are traced if deposited into a bank account.

What he did wrong... A growing number of eBayers are turning to cheque payments only because of the way PayPal often unfairly return buyers funds without the sellers consent. With cheque payments this is not possible. This trader only defrauded using cheques so PayPal were unable to trace or prove the funds. The problem this fraudster came across was that he defrauded too many people and received too many complaints for the 'authorities' to ignore. Arguably banks issuing cheques view fraud a little more seriously than PayPal does.

This person may well have got away with his crimes if he'd scaled the fraudulent cheque transactions down and continued to use PayPal honestly. The individual cheques were for small amounts and buyers may have lost interest in complaining to so many different authorities (Banks, PayPal, eBay, the Police and Internet Fraud Complaints Center) eventually.

Source: www.zwire.com New Haven Register•Com - By Neal Jones, Register Staff - Date: December 03, 2003

What eBay Isn't Telling You

In most fraud cases where a criminal 'gets away with it' the perpetrator gains the buyers trust before the fraud is executed. This is said to be the key to the perfect crime – if you do not have a criminal record, you don't get caught 'red handed' and you don't tell anyone what you are about to do, plus you just do it only once (don't get greedy), it is highly unlikely that you will get caught. Most bank robbers for instance are known to the police and have their finger prints and details on police records. In criminal history the people who execute the 'perfect crime' are thought to be people with no former convictions. If a model citizen chooses to do a crime and not get caught, it is advisable to do it big and do it only once. This way the chances of being caught are drastically cut.

In the following case the conman was able to gain large sums of money from eBay traders purely based on his reputation (good feedback). Unlike in the 'real world' where customers don't hand over large sums to people they do not know or have no contact details, eBay is a community that encourages false trust through the feedback system, which as we know is not accurate at all.

Five reports were compiled by the Internet Fraud Complaint Center (IFCC) and turned over to the local police force. Not a great deal of complaints one would conclude however, it was the size of each claim that alerted federal agencies. Each claim was between $1,000 and $20,000.

Police went to this fraudster's home and business to discuss this matter only to find that he had disappeared five days earlier leaving his wife with an empty bank account and some stiff questions to answer.

> The fact is if you are considering buying high end products from eBay their feedback system counts for nothing. In fact, good feedback can act as the backbone to a very lucrative scam and has been known that others will purchase from an account which has already built up a good reputation.

This person was able to get away because he used the fact that Police often take several days if not weeks to receive the crime complaint and to investigate it. By that time he was gone.

What he did wrong… Surely he should have taken his wife with him!

Source ; www.business2.com/authors/1,2110,918,00.html David H. Freedman

EBay account hijacking

Account hijacking might be more frequent than you'd think. Scammers crack an eBayers account password and use their "good sellers" reputation to draw unsuspecting buyers into purchasing non-existent products. The scammer changes the account password to prevent the real owner from logging on or contacting the buyers.

Often this fraud is conducted on short term auctions so a quick turnover is achieved before the authorities and police are able to put their coffee and donuts down and prevent the crime.

The victim found that he could not log-on to his eBay account and that someone had been offering Sony Camcorders for sale on his account. (At a price of $605 US).

Because all the products were offered on a one or three day auction the scammers were able to get the money and disappear before the account was shut down.

It must be said that many of the people scammed in this case were told to wire money by Western Union. EBay now clearly states to never use this system of payment due to the lack of identity it offers. Anyone with a password can collect the money from almost any city in the world proving it almost impossible to trace the fraudster. Those who used credit cards in this case were able to claim their money back.

As in the case above, the main problem in this case is that eBay failed to react quickly enough to the victim's complaints and transactions were already completed by the time eBay closed down the account.

Source: www.smh.com.au

What he did wrong... There is not much you can do to prevent this type of account hacking on eBay, other than to report it quickly to eBay. With the withdrawal of the one day listing in 2007 it is difficult to list an illegal item and disappear before eBay can investigate. Previously eBay took so long to look into claims that if listed in a one day auction the transaction could be complete before they looked into the complaint.

EBay con man sentenced

A Manchester (USA) man was fined $100, sentenced to four months in jail and a year of probation for an eBay scam in which he auctioned items he did not possess. He also had to pay back $4,500 of the stolen money.

The original products sold were Mobile phones which are easily sold as highly desirable and relatively expensive to buy. In addition this scammer claimed money back from the postal service for goods lost and told the buyers to do the same once they claimed that the goods had not arrived.

The high amount of fake tracking numbers that he created sealed this felon's fate.

A year went by and the scam continued, even following repeated warnings from the police to cease the illegal activities.

Source: www.ydr.com 0 Date: May 11, 2005

What he did wrong... This guy blundered all the way along. Again once the Police got involved and gave him a warning even the biggest idiot would stop the con. Once warned he could have got away with most of the money and given up. I'm sure even when this fraudster is released he will find himself back in trouble soon.

Huge non delivery eBay fraud

Salt Lake City Police arrested a man following hundreds of complaints by eBay buyers who failed to receive won goods. Trading under a company name the scammer took at least $1000 per victim for non- existent Laptop computers.

Police stated that it seems the fraudster profited from over $1 million in only a couple of weeks!

As with many such eBay frauds the scammer had knocked up hundreds of positive feedback before the scam was instigated. The company had a 'bricks and mortar' address but never actually traded in the real world; eBay was its sole source of income.

Again eBay didn't shut the account down until it was too late.

One of the most embarrassing aspects of this fraud is that the company partook in eBays SquareTrade seller verification service which gave potential customers the confidence to buy. Although SquareTrade is a third party site it is promoted as a part of the eBay group.

Source: MSNBC.com - By Bob Sullivan –Date: June 13, 2003

Original article: http://msnbc.com/news/925433.asp?0sl=-44&cp1=1

What he did wrong… Another greedy fraudster. If you are making Millions of dollars a year as this chap was, surely you put the funds into a legitimate business and stop the fraud before you end up in jail. Another idiot who needs to be locked up for his own safety as much as everyone elses!

Stolen car parts £32,000.

A sales manager was jailed for 12 months after admitting stealing car parts from his employers and selling them on eBay. The 23 year old from Southampton, England was jailed for 12 months.

The fraudster was a well paid Parts Manager for a car dealership so obviously had plenty of opportunity to access spare parts for resale. What he didn't account for was the established auditing system the company had in place that quickly saw through his attempts at altering the figures.

Due to the perpetrators good wage he was not in need of the extra income and duly gave the money back when caught, which was sitting in his bank account untouched.

England, Daily Echo. Julie Mcgee 2006

What he did wrong... It was inevitable that this character would be caught as the parts department that he worked and stole from had a system that flagged up discrepancies in stock. Although he fiddled the figures to hide his theft it was not a large enough extent.

This man didn't actually use the money he stole rather saved it in a bank account. He was then fortunate enough to be able to pay back the money once caught and avoid a longer sentence had he spent his ill gotten gains.

NINE

GREAT BIG Products you should avoid buying on eBay

PC Scanners and Printers from private sellers

Scanners are predominately made from glass and delicate electrical components; the likelihood of the product arriving from a private seller in one piece is very slim. Private sellers invariably don't have the packing skills or equipment for such a product and if they are intending to con you with an already broken product or swapping an old one then this product is ideal. Keep with the established bricks and mortar companies.

In addition the actual life span of such equipment is relatively low it is all to easy for a private seller to use the scanner/ printer whilst it is new and sell it just before it is worn out giving you a product that will only last a few months.

Online Auctioned Cars

Over Three Million visitors visit eBay Motors per month with a car being sold every two minutes.

EBay car buying used to be a minefield, this is changing because eBay bought in 'classified ads' for car sales which has changed the way it sells vehicles. The auction style format is still available but is arguably the most dubious style of online purchasing.

With classifieds the fees are paid by the car dealer and they start at £150 per month. The buyer does not pay through PayPal or eBay as the transaction is done in person with the dealer. This has cut down the problems eBay had before because lets face it you don't want to buy a car online that you have not seen. Bricks and Mortar car auctions have a reputation for being minefields for the uninitiated and you can look the cars around and even hear them run. Having online auctions just adds to the possibilities of buying a lemon.

With the new 'classifieds' at least you don't hand over any money until you have met the dealer and seen the car – this removes much of the risk. You also notice that the monthly fees for the classified style ads are quite high. Therefore, you can be reasonably assured that dealers who take part in this scheme are full time dealers, if they are prepared to shed out a monthly fee as high as this.

Products without a photo

The products photo does not need to be in the 'gallery' as this costs the seller more money, but there does need to be a photo of some description, or the seller should at least offer to email you one. If you have no photo you can't complain that the product is not what you wanted.

You must ask the seller to supply a photo and do it through eBay. That way, if the product once purchased does not match the photo you can get your money back or if they do not supply a photo you know it is probably dodgy.

DVD and CD's from private sellers

From my experience many CD's and DVD's are counterfeit copies and although copying of these is usually perfect due the advance in home computer technology if you want a real version it might be better to buy from a business seller. We've seen that if the product does not have a picture then it's best to keep away. And one aspect that is often over looked by buyers is the value of asking specific questions before the auction end. If the seller does not reply to the question – is this a real version or fake? Then it's almost certainly an illegal copy. If they say it is real but send you a fake you have more chance of a refund from PayPal.

EBay have a new policy that does not allow any DVD-R's or CD-R's to be listed on eBay unless the seller has the copyright. This is still impossible to regulate and even this week (May 2008) I was sold a fake CD, when I went to give bad feedback the owner closed his account. Sellers often close their accounts for a few weeks so buyers don't give them poor feedback then before the 50 day closure period ends reinstate their accounts and carry on trading. By this tie the conned buyer either forgets about the con or calms down and decides not to bother.

Electric downloads, Ebooks, PDF's etc

As mentioned earlier eBay will not guarantee these products in anyway. Even if the seller sells you a download and doesn't bother supplying it, eBay are not interested.

If you are a buyer don't bother. If you are a scammer with low moral standards - looking for a quick return – then this is an easy money spinner.

I have bought several electronic services from eBay and PayPal and was told that neither service would give me my money back for electronically supplied products or services in any circumstances.

Avoid at all costs unless you can afford to lose your money.

In April 2008 eBay changed their policy and now you can only sell a downloadable product in a 'classified' style listing. This may not last long or have much of an impact on downloadable rip offs.

Mobile phones

If they don't have a copy of the contract, a box and most importantly a charger then it's best to steer clear. So many mobile phones are stolen each year that eBay is an easy way for thieves to shift them – don't finance their dirty deeds.

There are legitimate 'bricks and mortar' mobile sellers on eBay but what's the point when you can simply go straight to the companies own website or into a shop.

This is another area eBay are changing. In 2007 an increase in listing fees for mobile phones was seen, which in theory prevents thieves from selling stolen phones. In reality the higher cost does not necessarily deter thieves as they have no overheads like real businesses- if they didn't realize thieves get their products for free eBay!!

Things to look out for before bidding

1. Check price comparison sites or large stores such as Amazon for values to get an indication if product is fake? If the price sounds too good it probably is. Ask specific questions through eBay so if there is a dispute when you receive the products eBay can see that the seller blatantly lied in response to your questions. This is

deliberate fraud so you are more likely to get your money back, although on eBay it is always a gamble!

2. Be careful and ensure that you can afford to purchase an item if after bidding someone else beats your price and you bid subsequently on another item. If the higher bidder drops out of the first auction you may end up buying both!

3. Have a separate credit card for PayPal or other online payment systems. If you get money stolen or PayPal try to give money back to a trader following a dispute that you don't agree to, they cannot take much out. If it's the account you have your wages paid into, PayPal could take as much as they wish. You can now get "pay as you go" credit cards that you top up when required. This is a great way to avoid having a lot of money, or even your credit card details stolen and PayPal can't whip money from you in a dispute.

4. If a seller has a large amount of low cost products in his history of sales then he may be setting up a good reputation in order to conduct a larger fraud. So avoid this person, they maybe buying themselves a reputation to create false trust.

5. Be aware of laws in other countries that you trade with. In USA federal law you are not allowed to be dishonest about your descriptions, shill bidding is prohibited and making false testimonials in the comments sections of eBay are not allowed. Although these are all regular occurrences on eBay and as we

have seen even eBay was prosecuted for shill biding themselves!

6. With the new fraud measures in England you may get prosecuted for illegal activity on eBay although this is probably only going to happen to the biggest con- artists.

7. Byelaws in America and England say you must ship within 30 days unless otherwise stated. How many people would actually get prosecuted for this is unknown.

How to keep ahead of the competition

1. Google Cart – So far Google are coming across as nice guys when it comes to their payment system. Rightly so, because they are coming into a competitive market. The other aspect that has to be realised about using Googles payment system is that they own the worlds most popular search engine. This may have an effect when listing your website in the years to come.

2. Don't use eBay / PayPal. Unfortunately until an online giant comes along to rival eBay it remains a massive source of traffic for selling to. Not using the site will cost you but there are ways to reduce your financial costs on eBay. Firstly use eBay as a Marketing platform for your website. Drive traffic to your site but do it within the eBay rules. Linking to your site from your "about me" page is allowed. And if you are discrete you'll easily get away with directing people to your site from your item descriptions if you tell potential customers to "see my website"

for more information.

3. EBay verse's your own site. You are eligible for a merchant account such as one with The Royal Bank of Scotland – WorldPay. Use a merchant account on your own website so the eBay con man cannot claim a PayPal dispute and get their money back. This may reduce the amount of customers you receive as PayPal are huge, but in the long run it will save you a lot of grief. If you use eBay solely without your own website and eBay ban you – you lose your online income, so cover yourself.

4. Use your eBay database to market to past customers through your own website.

5. Bid the price you want the product for then leave the auction site. If you do not win fine!

6. Use a pay-as-you-go credit card on eBay, if you get your details stolen they can only take out or use the small amount that you keep on the card.

7. Mark you items with infra-red codes, this will enable you to know if someone tries to swap your product with another and claim a refund. Make sure you take a photo of your product before dispatch this will aid your defense, you'll need to take photos anyway for the listing so you might as well take a photo of the code as well.

8. Optimise your listings in order to maximize it's exposure on eBay as well as Google. This dramatically increases traffic. And yes, this means keyword spamming on your eBay listing.
9. Use 10 day listings and finish them on a Sunday. Ten day listings create a four percent increase in sale price on average.

10. Don't get tied into a war of bidding – set your top price and walk away. If you don't get it then it is too expensive so you are OK. Wait for the next one.

11. Only accept cheques and postal orders. But let them clear before sending the product. Don't forget that this could still see you out of pocket if the bank decides to claim the money back if a fraudulent cheque is discovered. Be very wary if the cheque turns out to be more than the product sells for. It is almost guaranteed to be fake and you will lose the money.

12. Don't ever leave feedback until buyer/sellers leave feedback first – EVER! Nice people become psychopaths when they realise they have you over a barrel, all sorts of blackmail will come forward - POWER does nasty things to the weak, especially when they are apparently safe in their own home.

13. Sue eBay - Take out small claims for money owed.
People seem to be intimidated by big organizations such as eBay and avoid   suing them. This needn't be the case. With today's technology it only takes ten minutes to fill out a county court judgment online and the fee to do so is minimal. I hope, with the trend in suing banks for their default charges people are being to

understand the law a little bit more and become encouraged to take on these corporate giants legally. They are the ones who need to avoid adverse media publicity so they should be settling out of court as quickly as possible. Not just in an attempt to avoid poor media relations but to keep good customer satisfaction. If eBay or PayPal owe you money take them to court. It is simple as that. Watch their change in policy when a wave of disgruntled customers do the same.

14. Sue eBay traders- Take out small claims for money owed if someone refuses to send you your product back once a refund has been initiated. It is quicker and cheaper than you think. Most people don't want to be sued so will see the light and pay what they owe you if you take out a county court judgment. See the last chapter for website addresses.

TEN

GREAT BIG eBay Solutions

Employ more people – they have the funds!

Several years ago EBay lost a $35 million patent-infringement judgment. During the same year the 'Federal Trade Commission' had 51,000 complaints of fraud just on the US site.

Most of these complaints were for goods not received. It seems that eBay are incapable of regulating this problem themselves.

More recently on 1st July 2008 eBay were fined £30m by a French court for selling fake goods. EBay argued that they spend £10m a year keeping the site clean – it seems that this may not be enough?

They have the money to virtually fix any problem within eBay and that includes fraud. The truth is that it seems all the 'problems' that have not been addressed adequately are problems that are very profitable to eBay. Shill biding helps eBay make an enhanced fee. EBay are happy to promote items that are ending soon hence encouraging sniping.

There are other auction sites that check sold items to reduce postal fraud, sites that have a much lower financial turnover than eBay. EBay could even afford to run their own postal service - this would stop postal charge arguments or lost in post scams.

They could check all items that are in a dispute to ensure they are sent back to the seller when a refund is given. In fact such a service could be a huge benefit to eBay. They spend enough money buying out the auction site competition why not buy out or invest in a postal service that would track and guarantee a good service?

There are many unanswered questions with reference to trading on eBay. Such as the disclosure of the percentage of auctions that receive no bids. Why is this kept from the public unless of course, eBay make so much money in this manner they don't want to scare off the traders who re-list on a consistent basis? Or perhaps they have developed their listing facility so that many new eBayers mis-list and eBay receive relisting fees when products are not sold? Perhaps?

Source: Star-Telegram.com - Competition, fraud may harm eBay, By Wendy Tanaka, Date: July 5, 2003

Multiple bidding

EBay could stop multiple biding by not allowing multiple locations on accounts using the same IP address. We know they monitor IP addresses because PayPal send account holders a warning when an unfamiliar IP has been used to logon to an account.

Don't get involved in bidding wars

EBay need to accept that most of the business done on eBay is due to the psychological aspects of excitement and winning just like gambling. Sniping should not be considered an illegal activity as it forms most of the auctions and eBays income would be severely hit if it did not occur. In addition, having ridiculous laws such as this dilute the seriousness of other fraud because it is practiced to such a high degree on eBay. If eBay, foolishly, want to reduce shill biding then they need to take a leaf out of Amazon.com's book who have a much smaller degree of shilling.

As a consumer it is all too easy to get caught up in a bidding war. It's human nature, this is a part of the reason why eBay and other auction sites/ gambling sites are so successful.

Bid the price you want the product for then leave the auction site. If you do not win that's fine – you'll only regret it if you bid more than you wanted to! And lets face it, there are not many items that will not show up again on eBay as long as you are prepared to wait.

Reducing fraud with Free pictures

The fact is that if a product is on eBay which is easily duplicated on a home computer such as CD's and DVD's and the listing does not have a picture then it is likely to be a counterfeit. EBay realise this, but encourage users not to put multiple pictures on their listing as it will cost the seller more. By allowing free pictures eBay would be allowing buyers to see the product and make it far more difficult to send a fake. One rule is that the product being sold must be "as advertised". Without a picture it's difficult to complain.

In addition, the more photos you have the better you can represent your products condition. If you are penalised for adding more pictures people are less likely to add photos of scratches, worn out parts etc and the more likely it is that a buyer receives a product that is not as they hoped. EBay should allow users to add extra photos without punishing them financially, if they are keen to stop customer dissatisfaction.

From looking on eBay and studying the people who have got away with making hundreds of thousands of pounds annually until they were eventually prosecuted it is clear that the simplest way to con people on eBay is to sell non-existent products. Unlike the real world you don't have to have a product in stock to sell it. If you have higher moral standards than this there is still no reason why you shouldn't sell products you do not have and purchase them when sold to deliver.

Research your product

There is no better business skill than researching your product thoroughly. You can do this on and off eBay. We have discussed how to use the eBay 'advanced search' to establish selling prices of sold products before. You can also check other sites such as Amazon for product price, often being cheaper than eBay auctions. A useful tool if you are looking to buy and sell to make a profit.

Alternative Payment Systems

There are many different payment systems available on the web. But as an eBay company PayPal are set to remain the number one system on eBay. We've seen the problems you may encounter from crooks who make use of PayPal's eagerness to pay back money to buyers without much investigation. It will be difficult in the near future to sell on eBay without PayPal but certainly it is preferable to have a different system on your own website. Googles new cart seems like it could turn out to be a welcomed relief to the PayPal cart but only time will tell. Google at least, allow you to download money everyday if you wish. A dramatic improvements in PayPal's seven day download time.

Reduce your reliance upon eBay

As soon as you get a steady income from eBay build upon your own site, you will be eligible for a merchant account when you establish an income and banks such as The Royal Bank of Scotland will allow you to use their merchant account WorldPay.

Alternative Online Auction Sites

There are many 'alternative' auction websites all with there own pros and cons. Unfortunately none have the traffic that eBay enjoys. This said traffic is not everything, eBay in my opinion often has too many categories and your product becomes lost I the crowd. I believe specialist sites are the way forwards as you have fewer categories and the customer base is specific to your product.

General sites

www.oztion.com.au - an Australian auction site that many eBays have turned too.

http://www.auctionlotwatch.co.uk - Lists 56 alternative UK auction sites.

http://www.ebid.net - This site has no listing fee (so you have nothing to lose to give it a go). This is one of the largest alternative auction sites on the web.

http://www.ioffer.com - This site works very much like eBay and even lets you transfer your feedback from eBay, so you don't have to start all over again building an online reputation. Also allows the use of PayPal.

Specialist auction sites

http://www.model-auctions.com or http://www.thetoyauctioneer.com - Toys

http://www.delcampe.co.uk – a site for collectors

http://www.auctionkeyword.com - Helps you discover the most popular keywords on eBay.

http://www.vdepot.co.uk - EBay product warehousing and fulfillment services.

http://powersellersunite.com - Power sellers unite was "born" when eBay implemented rate increases that upset eBay sellers. This site now claims that its focus has now shifted away from the eBay boycott in early 2005 to helping sellers, and buyers, find the best alternative auction site(s) for their needs.

http://www.auctionhelpline.co.uk - Auction Helpline / Support

http://groups.google.com/group/auctionplease - Anti eBay user group that unites disgruntled eBayers to discover a new alternative to eBay. And particularly let Google know of their intentions.

Useful contacts in the event of Fraud against you.
Complaints in USA

http://www.fbi.gov/majcases/fraud/internetschemes.htm

The Internet Crime Complaint Center a partner of the FBI and the National White Collar Crime Center. – www.ic3.gov

www.fbi.gov/whitecollarcrime.htm

National white collar crime centre - www.nw3c.org

Useful Agencies

Trading Standards Counterfeiting Hotline

Trading Standard's Counterfeiting Hotline which you can contact in confidence and pass on any information you have. They will investigate and take action where appropriate.

To contact the hotline call: **0121 303 9367.**

UK - Office of fair trading.

http://www.oft.gov.uk/news/press/2007/155-07

Informs consumers of their rights under the Distance Selling Regulations (DSRs). They also inform businesses that using auction sites as a sales channel requires them to adhire to legal obligations under the E-Commerce Regulations (ECRs).

The Consumer Protection from Unfair Trading Regulations 2007, implements the EU's Unfair Commercial Practices Directive and prohibits businesses from treating consumers unfairly. It obliges businesses not to use:

- aggressive practices
- misleading practices

One of the key tests in the regulations is whether the unfair commercial practice in question materially distorts the consumer's economic behaviour (e.g. was the consumer persuaded to make a purchase they wouldn't otherwise have made because of the commercial practice?).

A breach of the Consumer Protection from Unfair Trading Regulations 2007 is, in most cases, a criminal offence. Find out more from BERR about the Unfair Commercial Practices Directive.

The Department for Business Enterprise and Regulatory Reform (BERR).

Make sure your listings are not misleading – Unfair Commercial Practices Directive.

Unfair Commercial Practices Directive

http://www.berr.gov.uk/consumers/buying-selling/ucp/index.html

The Unfair Commercial Practices Directive (UCPD) was adopted on 11 May 2005. Consumer Protection from Unfair Trading Regulations implementing the Directive in the UK will come in to force on 26 May 2008.

The Consumer Protection from Unfair trading Regulations repeal provisions in a number of overlapping laws, including most of the Trade Descriptions Act 1968 and Part 3 of the Consumer Protection Act 1987 (misleading price indications).

The Consumer Protection Act 1987 makes it a criminal offence to give consumers a **misleading price indication about goods**, services, accommodation (including the sale of new homes) or facilities.

Distance Selling Regulations

Distance selling means selling and buying by phone, mail order, via the **Internet** or digital TV. Such transactions are covered generally by normal buying and selling legislation, but they are also covered by special Distance Selling Regulations.

Distance Selling Regulations give protection to consumers who shop by phone, mail order, via the Internet or digital TV: The protection includes:

• The right to receive clear information about goods and services before deciding to buy;
• Confirmation of this information in writing;
• A cooling off period of seven working days in which the consumer can

withdraw from the contract;
- Protection from credit card fraud.

USA Attorney Generals office in your state.

Consumer Protection Agency - http://www.consumerprotectionagency.co.uk

The Federal Trade Commission - www.ftc.gov

The Copyright Licensing Agency Ltd. - http://www.cla.co.uk

The Creators' Rights Alliance (CRA) - http://media.gn.apc.org/ccindex.html

Office of Public Sector Information - http://www.opsi.gov.uk

Internation Trademark Association - http://www.inta.org

Community Watch — Community members can report prohibited, questionable and infringing items to eBay.

PayPal discussion forums

http://www.sfgate.com/cgi-bin/article.cgi?file=/chronicle/archive/2002/09/07/BU232114.DTL&type=business#sections.

www.PayPalSucks.com - PayPal Sucks is an anti PayPal site that highlights the problems with PayPal.

www.PayPalWarning.com – PayPal Horror Stories. - This site provides warning of PayPal problems in advance. Including questions;

www.AboutPayPal.org - Another site highlighting PayPal issues.

http://www.rebel101.com/sue_PayPal.htm - A site discussing how the owner sued PayPal and won.

http://attrition.org/~squido/PayPal - Online Article – 'How PayPal is the Biggest of Online Scammers'.

http://www.marketwatch.com - WASHINGTON (CBS.MW) -- Online payment service PayPal agreed to pay $150,000 to New York's attorney general to settle charges the company misrepresented its policies to accountholders.

The Law

The Sale of Goods Act 1979 - sellers are responsible for ensuring that any goods they sell on eBay are: in accordance with the description they have given in the item listing; of satisfactory quality; and fit for their purpose.

The Trade Descriptions Act 1968 - makes it an offence for sellers to: apply a false description to any items; or supply or offer to supply any items to which a false description is applied.

Trading Standards CD duplication policy?

Software piracy is the duplication, distribution or use of software without authorization from the copyright owner. This includes actions like:

- Downloading unlicensed copies of software from the internet.

- Making copies for (or loaning disks to) friends.

- Installing one licensed copy onto multiple computers.

- Selling unlicensed or counterfeit copies online or elsewhere.

- Using unlicensed or counterfeit copies.

And when it comes to distributing software to others, it doesn't matter whether that distributing is done for profit or not. It's still illegal.

Afterword

Although there appears to be a mass of problems on eBay, there is hope. The intention of this book is certainly not to encourage traders to act unlawfully, or to try to con and be dishonest on eBay or elsewhere. That resides within the individual and their own moral standards.

I am hoping that rather then spend millions of dollars more on buying up their competition eBay will spend more on developing ways to make their site safer – especially for the 'newbie'.

I am optimistic that a giant such as Google will step in with an alternative to eBay forcing them to become more competitive and making them safer. This does seem to be the case with Google and eBay becoming more and more similar. EBay turning into a giant shopping search engine and Google with the largest online advertising system in the world selling other peoples products. I hope this continues, forcing eBay into better practices, perhaps more along the good service model Amazon manages to operate, even with its third party section.

Even after researching and practicing some of the cons found in this book I am still not immune to eBay swindles. Only this week I bought a DVD which turned out to be fake. Leave bad feedback and alert eBay I hear you say. Well, when I went to the feedback section I discovered that the seller had cancelled his account. I will keep an eye out over the next few weeks because as we know once cancelled you can reinstate your account again within 50 days. I suspect the trader may do this once he feels his victims will have given up on trying to leave feedback. Alternatively, he'll probably just start another account!

The reason I wrote this book was because of my frustration at being conned on eBay. Also, that such a giant company with masses of revenue available, still seems reluctant to address this situation satisfactorily and seem to be to be more interested in profit than customer satisfaction. I believe the only reason some of the 'illegal' practices that blight eBay are allowed to carry on is because if stopped eBay would lose profit. In my opinion that's the only logical reason I can see in letting it carry on.

The other reason for this book is my concern at the sheer number of traders willing to commit crimes on eBay without any sense of guilt. A whole generation appears to have been bought up to steal from other traders without remorse. They are becoming desensitized to the effects of theft by hiding behind a computer screen. Many wouldn't dream of stealing from a 'bricks and mortar' shop as the consequences would be far more immediate if caught. The feedback system championed as being a failsafe way to regulate the quality of customer service simply does not work. In fact we've seen it can do exactly the opposite to its intended purpose. Blackmail and extortion are easy within the system.

Fraud or not, simply put, eBay offers a huge market place where thousands of pounds can be made by the shrewd trader. However, it does seem that most successful traders need to 'learn the hard way' before they get to grips with techniques to protect themselves.

In late April 2008 Microsoft 'threatened' Yahoo to voluntarily sell their site to them or they will take over aggressively and probably for less than they were offering. It seems then, that a shake up of the Giants is inevitable and perhaps Google and eBay will be forced to retain their partnerships to close ranks on Microsoft? As off My 2008 Microsoft claim they are no longer interested in Yahoo. That sounds doubtful and is probably a tactical manoeuvre to get Yahoo cheaply.

1ST May 2008 saw another 'strike' of eBayers. This time it was UK traders who held a one day strike to communicate their grievances against fee changes and Powersellers increased benefits. It seems the advent of a new Chief executive has seen many changes to eBay that independent traders are not happy about. These include feedback problems, fee changes and particularly bias's towards large company's who trader on eBay.

The new CEO at eBay is making many changes and they seem to going in the right direction. Feedback has changed to such an extent that it might actually start representing a traders reputation, that would be nice!

EBay is here to stay. Lets' hope they sort out the bad apples and make trading safer and more enjoyable - only time will tell.

About the Author

Authorpreneur and research psychologist Steve has had over 60 books and sports hypnosis CD's published.

It was in the marketing of these products that Steve was dragged in to the murky world of online auctions and forced to defend his products from unscrupulous traders. Steve has been researching the behaviour of online traders for over two years.

In the real world Steve has over a decade of experience in Sports and Mind Therapies utilizing psychology and hypnosis.

A former University boxer and dedicated athlete Steve's best selling Sports Hypnosis CD's have helped to inspire, develop and motivate athletes worldwide. More information about Steve and the work that he does can be found at the following websites.

www.The-eBay-Con.co.uk

www.SportsHypnosis.co.uk

ISBN: 978-0-9558533-0-2

Printed in the UK

In association with Lulu.com

Printed in the United Kingdom
by Lightning Source UK Ltd.
135348UK00002B/329/P